Stone Shelters

Stone Shelters

Edward Allen

The MIT Press Massachusetts Institute of Technology Cambridge, Massachusetts, and London, England

ISBN 0 262 01027 5 (hardcover)

ISBN 0 262 51010 3 (paperback)

Library of Congress catalog card number: 74-76447

ai miei amici italiani

Preface

Stone Shelters is a history of the making of buildings, and of the combining of these buildings into towns, in a small, geographically well-defined area of southern Italy known as the Murgia of the Trulli. Its primary purpose is to gain an understanding of a vernacular architecture as it relates to the geography of a land and the history of its people. It is not intended as a glossy picture book or a clever sketchbook, but rather as a documentation of how various types of buildings and towns have arisen in response to particular geographic, social, political, and economic conditions. It is not intended as a catalog of beautiful architectural forms, but instead as a study of how architectural forms come into being.

Its first chapter begins with a brief discussion of the basic geography, history, and folklore of the Murgia of the Trulli and the surrounding region of Apulia. In the second chapter, the roots of the buildings of the Murgia are traced to other times and to other areas of Apulia. The succeeding three chapters, the heart of the book, describe in detail the three mature types of buildings in which the inhabitants of the Murgia housed themselves and from which the towns of the Murgia were built: manmade caves, *trulli*, and buildings vaulted with stone and mortar. For each building type an exemplary town is examined in depth. The concluding chapter considers the formal implications of the twentieth-century materials and techniques of construction which are now in use on the Murgia. Particular emphasis is given throughout the book to the degree of responsiveness of each building technique to the needs of those who built with it. The suitability of each technique for the making of towns is also considered.

This project was begun with the partial support of a study grant for the academic year 1966–1967 which was given by the United States Department of State under the Fulbright-Hays Act. This grant was obtained with the assistance of gracious recommendations by Robert Bliss, Donlyn Lyndon, Charles W. Moore, Ralph Rapson, William Turnbull, Jr., and Richard R. Whitaker, Jr. Through the patient efforts of Barbara Horwich Lloyd and Renata Poole, the author's knowledge of Italian was brought to a level sufficient to begin the research. Many potential difficulties in Italy were effectively eliminated by the staff of the Commissione Americana per gli Scambi Culturali con l'Italia, especially Cipriana Scelba, Luigi Filadoro, Silva Valier, and Gianna Zanetti. Mrs. Lisa Ronchi Torossi was a valued advisor and a source of much encouragement during the entire progress of the work. Giorgio Simoncini and Bruno Zevi contributed expert advice at several critical times.

The field work in Apulia depended heavily on the kindness, patience, and unselfishness of many dozens of individual inhabitants of stone shelters, most of whose names were unfortunately never recorded. In Alberobello, the Ufficio Pro Alberobello and the Ufficio Tecnico were of special assistance.

In Cisternino, Tenente Nicolo De Cantis and his entire police force were enthusiastic and helpful supporters of this research. Sacerdote Saverio Ostuni gave generously of his hard-earned knowledge of the town and its history. Pietro Punzi was an expert guide and a welcome companion. Quirico Punzi, schoolteacher, historian, and archeologist, was an invaluable source of historical data and an opener of many doors. Geometro Vincenzo Punzi, Pietro's father, and Sarto Vincenzo Punzi, Quirico's father, contributed much valuable information to the study. Ingegner Giovanni Sabatino, in addition to his services as an expert source of information concerning techniques of construction, assisted the author and his wife in finding lodgings for an extended stay in Cisternino. Vincent Scarafile was a constant help in the research effort, an able translator in difficult situations, and remains a warm personal friend. Anna Za was a willing chauffeur and a kind and patient assistant during some of the measuring of houses. Angelo Zizzi, whom the author scarcely knew, devoted many hours of effort to an ill-fated attempt to arrange for the taking of aerial photographs.

The full extent of the cave town at Massafra was very nearly overlooked by the author; Jack, Nita, Philip, Sara, and Naomi Goldstein, Michael Cooke, and Harvey and Ellen Schorr were the adventuresome companions who turned a casual visit to the Gravina of the Madonna della Scala into a major exploratory effort.

Irwin Welcher of General Graphic Services in San Francisco gave much more effort, expertise, and understanding to the production of the photographic enlargements than appeared on his invoices.

The author's mother, Mildred Allen, and his wife's parents, Arthur and Virginia Mennes, assisted the research in innumerable tangible ways, as well as by their constant interest and encouragement.

The author's wife, Mary, was a full working partner in all of the field study. She took more than a year from her own professional life and gave it enthusiastically and without reservation to the work which is here reported. It was through her suggestion that the full scope of this volume was realized, and it was through her interest, encouragement, and assistance that it was carried to completion.

Contents

Stone Shelters

I

The Stone Sponge

In the year 1717 the philosopher George Berkeley set out from Naples to visit an obscure corner of Italy called Apulia. He was among the first gentlemen of his time to make such a journey, for bandits still harassed travelers along the southern Italian roads, and Turkish pirates still made frequent raids along the Adriatic coast. Despite these hazards, he returned unscathed to Naples four weeks later, claiming to have viewed in Apulia the most beautiful cities in the world.[1]

Apulia, the "*fortunata terra di Puglia*" of Dante's poem, is today of much easier access. Its charms have not diminished since Berkeley's time. Yet it remains an obscure region, little known even to Italians, geographically apart from the well-worn paths of trade, tourism, and scholarly interest.

The southwestern boundary of Apulia is the Apennine Range. Its long northeastern edge is the Adriatic coast. Its southernmost extremity is the heel of the Italian boot, the Salentine Peninsula, which divides the Adriatic Sea from the Ionian Sea and the Gulf of Taranto. It stretches northwestward to include the spur of Italy, the Gargano Massif, a mammoth lump of rock projecting from the sea. Its northern plain, Capitanata, is vast and fertile, well suited to the growing of grain. Its seacoasts are backed with flat, broad plains, now lush grey-green matrices of olive trees. A single sluggish river, the Ofanto, called Aufidus by the Romans, crosses its middle. Its interior, behind the coastal plains, is a chain of three high, rocky plateaus called in Italian *murge*: the Northern Murgia, the Murgia of the Trulli, and the Salentine Murgia to the south.

The Murgia of the Trulli, the middle of the three, an oblong stone terrace wedged into the base of the Italian heel, is the focus of this study. It was on this *murgia*, compact and geographically well defined, that all the vernacular architectural experimentations of Apulia reached their highest levels of development. It was here that manmade caves, hewn from solid stone, became living cave towns in Byzantine times. It was here that the *trulli*, built of unmortared limestone, developed into year-round habitations and communities under the oppression of petty feudal despotism. It was here, too, that fortified cities were built of mortared stone, utilizing to the full the ingenious vocabulary of vaulting which was assembled in the Gothic era.

The surface of the Murgia of the Trulli, gently undulating, lies in elevation between 1,300 and 2,000 feet above the level of the sea. Its length is roughly forty miles and its width about twenty-five. Its long northeastern side drops off precipitously to the Adriatic plain below. To the south, toward the Gulf of Taranto, the Murgia slopes away more gently, and its edge is deeply serrated by numerous dry ravines, cut by water in ancient times. To the northwest lies the barren northern Murgia.

The Murgia of the Trulli is a great sponge of stone, for it has no ponds, lakes, streams, or rivers. It does not shed or hold water, but absorbs it. Its surface is a series of shallow, closed basins which funnel the rainfall into fissures in the thick underlying layer of white limestone, from which, by long underground labyrinths, it is eventually conducted beneath the surrounding coastal plains to emerge again from springs at the shore.

Originally the limestone layer of the Murgia, up to 7,500 feet in thickness, was flat and impervious. Small irregularities in its surface trapped and held pools of rainwater. But the water, slightly acid from carbon dioxide absorbed during its passage through the air, ate away chemically at the limestone over a period of many thousands of years, gradually forming the shallow basins and seeping its corrosive way through faults in the stone to produce the fissures and subterranean passages.[2] One can easily distinguish the various basins which comprise the countryside of the Murgia, and the fissures at their bottoms are often marked by protective stone walls, or by green clumps of moisture-seeking wild shrubbery. At Putignano and Castellana Grotte, two such fissures and their underground caverns, resplendent with gleaming multicolored stalactites and stalagmites, have been developed for tourism and can be explored by anyone paying the price of admission. They are among the most spectacular natural limestone caves in Europe.

Some of the basins are found filled with a red soil called *bolo*, a product of the decomposition of the limestone which is rich in hydroxides of iron and calcium. The rest of the surface of the Murgia is sparsely covered with a few shallow inches of rock-filled organic soil.

At its southern edge, where the Murgia slopes upward from the flat plain of the shoreline, its limestone layer is encircled by a deep band of *tufo*, an extremely soft, sandstonelike, homogeneous sedimentation of volcanic debris and mollusk shells. It is from *tufo* that the now-dry ravines, called *gravine*, were eroded. *Tufo* is extensively quarried in modular blocks for building construction. Like the limestone, when quarried it is nearly white in color, but it darkens and hardens somewhat on exposure to the elements. It is from these two stones, limestone and *tufo*, that the Murgia has earned the nickname *Puglia Pietrosa*, Rocky Apulia. Yet, perhaps encouraged by the early springtimes, the sunny warmth of the summers, and the abundant rainfall of the winters, oak forests and grasslands once managed to grow on the scarce soil, making the Murgia suitable for hunting and for the pasturing of animals.

Apulia has been inhabited since very early times. In the Grotta Romanelli, near Otranto, evidence of a protolithic culture has been found. Remains of a paleolithic village twenty to twenty-five thousand years old have been discovered at Torre Testa, on the Adriatic coast near Brindisi. Trade between Apulia and countries of the Aegean Sea has taken place since at least the second millenium B.C. The earliest discovered evidence of population on the Murgia of the Trulli, however, dates only from twelve to fifteen centuries before Christ. Probably there was little reason to inhabit the Murgia until the richer coastal plains became crowded. When colonization did take place the settlers did not ascend the steep cliff facing the Adriatic, but rather the gentle southern slope. In the Age of Bronze, numerous pastoral settlements dotted the southern area of the Murgia. Cattle, horses, sheep, and swine were raised, wool was spun, and decorated pottery was made.[3]

The earliest recognizable tribes of Apulia are known only as names: Siculi, Ausoni, Chones, Morgeti. Later the Iapygians migrated from the north of Italy and settled in Apulia. Subgroups developed within the Iapygians: the Daunians in northern Apulia, and the Peucetians in the central region, including part of the Murgia of the Trulli. The Salentine Peninsula, including the southeastern portion of the Murgia of the Trulli, was inhabited by another tribe, the Messapians. According to Pliny, the Messapians were the descendents of nine youths and nine maidens of the Illyrians. In later times the Romans called the Iapygians *Apuli* and from this gave the region its name. The Salentine Peninsula and the neighboring region of Calabria took their titles from the Salentine and Calabrian subgroups which the Romans identified within the Messapian tribe.[4]

The Mycenaeans founded early colonies in Apulia on both the Adriatic and Ionian shores. Later, in 706 B.C., the city of Taranto, christened Taras by the Greeks, was founded by colonists from Sparta. Its relations with the native tribes were not the best; dedications at Delphi record warfare against both the Messapians and Peucetians, and in the year 473 B.C. the Tarentines were overwhelmed and slaughtered by the Iapygians. A recovery was made, however, for in time virtually all the major Iapygian cities came under an uneasy Greek control, including the capital of Peucetia at Monte Sannace, near the present-day town of Gioia del Colle on the Murgia of the Trulli.[5]

In 342 B.C. King Archidamus II of Sparta was asked to come to the aid of the Tarentines because of continuing difficulties with the neighboring tribes. After a three-year campaign he was defeated and killed. Alexander of Epirus, cousin of Alexander the Great, came as avenger and subdued not only the Messapians, but the nearby Lucanians, Bruttians, and Samnites as well. Where Archidamus had died because of his military failure, Alexander died for another reason entirely: The Tarentines assassinated him when his spreading conquests began to assume the look of a personal empire which might threaten the sovereignty of Taras.[6]

Meanwhile, the Romans had become involved in Apulian affairs. In 307 B.C. the resurgent Samnite tribe of the southern Apennine valleys waged a successful campaign against the Romans on Apulian soil. In the following year Rome struck back and recaptured her Apulian territory. In 302, Rome sided with the Messapians against the Tarentines and their newest champion, the Spartan prince Cleonymus.

In wars of 326 and 299 B.C., the Peucetians were allied with the Romans against the Greeks. During the Third Samnite War, in 296 B.C., the Roman army under Decius Mus plundered an Apulian town called Murgantia, perhaps the source of the word *murgia*.[7]

In the year 280 B.C., the death struggle of the Greek colonies in Apulia began. Yet another champion, the Spartan king Pyrrhus of Epirus, arrived with troops and elephants. He was devastatingly effective. After defeating a Roman consular army in Basilicata, he marched to within forty miles of Rome, then turned southward again. In 279, he again conquered Roman forces at Asculum in northern Apulia, and made an inconclusive treaty with Rome before hurrying to the aid of the Greek colonies in Sicily. Unfortunately for the Greeks, as Pyrrhus was spending the last of his resources in Sicily, the Romans were quietly retaking control of Apulia. When in 275 Pyrrhus abandoned an unsuccessful campaign in Sicily and returned to Italy, he was soundly beaten by the Roman army at Beneventum. By 272 B.C., the Greeks were driven from Taras, and Rome reigned in all of Apulia.[8]

Apulia, together with Calabria comprising Region II of Italy in Augustus's scheme, developed rapidly for two centuries under Roman domination, grew in population and wealth, and gradually lost its former Eastern flavor as it adopted Roman ways. For the Romans, Apulia was the key to eastward trade and expansion. From the year 170 B.C. the Via Appia connected Rome to the harbor at Brindisi. The Via Traiana ran from Rome through northern Apulia to the water's edge at Bari. From these two superb natural ports of Apulia sailed the Roman fleets to Macedonia, Greece, Asia Minor, Syria, and Egypt, and up the highways to Rome flowed the riches of the East.[9]

Although Apulia remained Roman until the fall of the Empire, even these were not entirely peaceful times. In addition to sporadic civil insurrections, the Romans were faced with a threat from without in the person of Hannibal of Carthage.

Hannibal had made his famous crossing of the Alps in 218 B.C., and had marched southward almost to the gates of Rome, only to be trapped by a Roman army under Fabius. Hannibal's army had escaped the trap at night, and after another brief military foray in the vicinity of Rome, had withdrawn to Apulia for the winter. It was there in 216 B.C. that they captured the Roman supply depot at Cannae on the southern bank of the Aufidus. In June of that year, the Romans arrayed 87,200 of their best troops against 50,000 Carthaginians in an attempt to regain Cannae. The Romans were drawn into a pincer movement by Hannibal, and lost about 50,000 of their number in one terrible day of defeat.

Three years later, after indifferent success in southern Italy, and reinforced by troops of Philip of Macedon, an uncle of Pyrrhus of Epirus, Hannibal took Roman Tarentum, the Greek Taras, on his second attempt. His main garrison at Capua, near Naples, was constantly besieged by the Romans, however, and he was twice forced to return there to attempt a rescue. It was on his second mission to Capua that he drove rapidly to within five miles of the city of Rome, hoping to draw away the troops laying siege to Capua. Sneaking back, he found to his chagrin that the Romans still surrounded Capua. Eventually the Romans prevailed, and Tarentum fell as well in 209 B.C. Hannibal's brother Hasdrubal, who had crossed the Alps and was making steady military progress down the Italian peninsula, was unexpectedly captured and killed. Any remaining Carthaginian threat to Roman power now collapsed and, in 203 B.C., Hannibal returned by ship to Carthage.

After the eventual fall of imperial Rome, few of the northern barbarian conquerors harassed Apulia. It instead came under Byzantine control. The Byzantines managed to retain possession of the land in the Gothic-Byzantine War of 535 to 553 A.D., but during the years of fighting the countryside was ravaged and the population decimated, and what little was left to the victors was taken away for the enrichment of Byzantium. In the year 590, the Longobards, attacking from the north, began capturing Apulian territory, and left the Byzantines holding only the lower half of the Salentine Peninsula after the wars of 662 to 667 A.D. For many years wars flared sporadically between these two powers. The countryside fell into ruin and there was little navigation of the seas. Apulia was in the darkest of times.

In the ninth century outsiders began to join in the still continuing squabble. German emperors, Dalmatian slave pirates, and Saracens raided the region. The Saracens captured Bari in 840 and Taranto in 842. Ludwig II of Germany took Bari in 871 after a three-year siege, but the Byzantines under Basil I regained it four years later and went on to capture most of Apulia from the Saracens and Longobards. For two centuries, during wars with Longobard princes, the popes, the German emperors Otto I and Otto II, and the Saracens, the Byzantines somehow kept control, even managing to establish trade ties between Apulia and Venice, Amalfi, and Dalmatia. Then, in the eleventh century, the Normans arrived in Apulia.

Centuries earlier, about the year 490 A.D., high in the mountains of Gargano, the Archangel Michael had appeared to the Bishop of Siponto in a cave.[10] This cave, despite its having been pillaged by sundry invaders, had grown steadily in riches and renown, and had become a sacred objective for Christian pilgrims from all over Europe. On such a pilgrimage came a handful of Norman soldiers in the early eleventh century. In 1015 they were taken as allies by Pope Benedict VIII against the Byzantines. Despite early victories, three years later the Normans were decisively beaten at Cannae.

In 1038, under the Hautevilles, the Apulian fortunes of the Normans began to turn. By 1043, Prince Waimar V of Salerno was able to proclaim himself Duke of Apulia and Calabria, and to give to William Ironarm of Altavilla the title Count of Apulia. In 1047, Apulia was given to the Normans as a fief by

Emperor Henry III. A Norman malcontent, Robert Guiscard, deprived of his share of this prize, moved southward to conquer Calabria for himself, then returned in 1053 to help rescue Apulia from Henry III, Pope Leo IX, and local Apulian rebels, allied to stamp out the menacing Norman ambition in Italy. The Pope was promptly captured by the Normans on Gargano, and in 1059 reconciled himself to Norman demands and named Guiscard Duke of Apulia, Calabria, and Arab-held Sicily. Guiscard soon initiated a re-enactment of his own story of twelve years earlier by expelling from Apulia without so much as a horse the young Norman nobleman Roger. Roger stole a horse, rallied an army, and conquered Sicily.

In 1071, the tenacious Byzantines were finally dislodged from their last Apulian outposts, Bari and Brindisi. Guiscard some years later started off to capture Byzantium itself, but in 1084 had to turn back to rescue Pope Gregory VII from a siege laid by Emperor Henry IV in Rome. Once the Pope was safe, the Norman troops, to make the excursion worthwhile, pillaged Rome before turning again toward Byzantium. It was on this second trip toward Byzantium that Guiscard died, at Corfu, in 1085. His heart was taken to the cathedral of Otranto, and his body to Venosa.

In 1095 Guiscard's son Boemond joined the First Crusade. He founded the first crusader state of Antioch and took the title of prince. Despite many attempts, he was unable to capture Byzantium, and in 1111 was buried at Canosa di Puglia in the tomb which still stands there bearing the single, proud inscription "Boamundus."

In 1127 Apulia, its throne abandoned, became part of the Sicilian kingdom of the Norman Roger II. It continued to grow in wealth. Yet all was not calm, for in 1156 William II leveled Bari as punishment for native insurrections which had been rooted there. Under William II, Norman power grew: Tancred of Lecce became the commander of the Norman fleet and conquered much of the eastern Mediterranean.[11]

On William's death, Apulia fell to the Hohenstaufens. The Norman times had been good ones for Apulia. The Crusades had filled its roads with travelers and its harbors with ships bound for the Holy Land. On its shores, under the patronage of the Normans and built with the superb skills of the Middle East, rose cathedrals that still rank among the most magnificent of the world.

Under the Hohenstaufen emperor Frederick II, Apulia continued to flower. Trade, art, and agriculture were further encouraged, and imposing castles were built on many Apulian hilltops. After Frederick's death, however, control passed in 1266 to Charles I of Anjou, who ruled from the throne at Naples, and once again Apulian fortunes went into a decline, reaching a low point under the Aragonese kings who took the throne in 1442. Feudalism became the law of the land. The once-rich sea trade was sold off as concessions to Venice, Florence, and Genoa.

Soon the Turks began making raids on this unhappy region, and captured Otranto in 1480. Then, taking advantage of continued warring between France and Spain over the Neapolitan throne, they sacked the entirety of Apulia. The French and Spaniards drove out the Turks, did some sacking of their own, and went on fighting between themselves. In 1503, Spain finally gained full control, and sponsored the extension of feudalism until the year 1707, when a Bourbon dynasty was established in Naples and the fortunes of Apulia began once again to rise. In 1799, however, this reign ended, plunging the region into a confused six decades of fighting among French, Spaniards, Royalists, and Italian patriots, which ended with the vote for Italian unification of 1860. Even then, for a decade afterward, Royalist brigands continued to keep the region in upheaval, until finally they too were killed or driven out.[12]

Today, in many isolated corners of the Murgia of the Trulli, people do not live much differently than did their ancestors a thousand years ago. Many still speak only the local dialects. At Massafra, *Massafrese* is spoken; at Alberobello, *Alberobellese*; at Cisternino, *Cisterninese*. Alberobello is only eleven miles from Cisternino and about fifteen from Massafra, but the dialect-speaking inhabitants of the three towns understand each other only with difficulty. Dozens of such dialects, propagated and maintained through the centuries of local feudal isolation, draw their root words in varying proportions from the languages of the conquerors of Apulia: Greek, Latin, Arabic, Longobard, English, German, French, Spanish. In some parts of the Salentine Peninsula almost pure Greek and Albanian are spoken.[13]

Farming is the main occupation on the Murgia, grapes and olives the primary crops. Wheat, *fave* beans, tomatoes, and other small crops are often cultivated among the olive trees. Figs and almonds are grown in many localities, and occasionally peach or apricot trees will be found. Table wines, neutral base wines for the making of vermouth, almonds, and olive oil are the main export products. Horses and mules provide motive power for the high-wheeled carts and the hand plows. Mechanization has reached many parts of the Murgia in the form of small hand tractors, three-wheeled motorscooter trucks, and tiny automobiles or motorcycles; but the fields are usually small, the stone-walled country lanes extremely narrow, and the tasks, such as the pruning of vines and trees or cultivation of very rocky soil, are often not adaptable to mechanization. Large-scale agricultural machinery is rarely seen.

Some parts of the Murgia, particularly the more rocky ones, are still given to pastureland, most often for sheep. Dairy cattle, goats, and swine are less common. Rabbits and chickens are often raised in dooryards to supply the family table, and the hunting of small game supplements the diet in many households.

The food and wines of the Murgia are among its greatest delights. Brick ovens fired with olive prunings yield hot bread and thick, steaming *focaccia*, topped with olive oil, large-crystal salt, and small tomatoes. Tiny ear-shaped *orecchiette* pasta catch in their shells and transport to the mouth the delicious sauces that are poured over them. Dried *fave* beans are hulled, boiled, and mashed, covered with olive oil, and carried hot to the table to blend their nut-like flavor with that of the dark, slightly bitter *verdura* greens which are served alongside. Thick rich *minestrone* is heaped high and fragrant in the bowl. Rolled veal *involtini* are smothered under a savory red sauce on the plate. Sliced roast veal is gently flavored with olive oil, salt, pepper, and bay leaves. Lamb entrails are skilfully made into tiny, spiced *gnumaredd* rolls. Eggplant and zucchini are sliced, breaded, stuffed, and cooked in dozens of different ways, each one better than the last. Local cheeses, fresh and aged, decorate the board, together with various sausages, and dessert is furnished by the fresh fruits of the region. Each town has its various wines, *rosso*, *rosato*, and *bianco*, each with its own distinctive flavor. In the countryside nearly every farmstead has giant stoneware jars, filled with its own wines from the previous season, hidden away in cool rooms to be brought out at mealtime by the brimming pitcherful. The most fortunate of guests in a household in the Murgia may be treated to a tiny glassful of homemade liqueur, a blend of pure alcohol, sugar, and fresh flavor of fruit or coffee; or to a portion of *vino cotto*, a strong flavorful wine made from boiled-down grape juice.

Catholicism is the nominal religion, and all profess to be Catholic, but church attendance is poor. For many, Sundays must be days of labor in the fields, especially for those who have other work and are only part-time farmers. Then, too, many remnants of mystical religions survive in Apulia: a belief in the power of one who has the "evil eye"; the use of mystical incantations, signs, and amulets; the dancing of the *tarantella*. Even within the framework of Catholicism there exist annual festivals which have all the external trappings of ancient pagan fertility rites.

By incredibly hard labor the Murgia of Trulli has been transformed from one of the least promising landscapes in the world into a rich garden, and its inhabitants are beginning to reap their rewards. New houses, automobiles, and appliances are owned by growing numbers of people. Even the less fortunate own their land and their houses, eat well, and keep their surroundings clean and in good repair. There is none of the desperate, dirty poverty which is occasionally seen in other parts of Italy, or in the United States; indeed, some outward signs of affluence are already creeping into the towns and the countryside.

Recent developments in Apulia promise a greater prosperity. Tentative drillings for petroleum are being made along the Adriatic coast. New superhighways, including one named La Panoramica which will cross the hilltops of the Murgia of Trulli, will bring Apulia into better contact with the commercial and recreational traffic of Italy. The Cassa del Mezzogiorno is furnishing money for the construction of new industries such as the giant Italsider steel mill which is already in operation near Taranto. Even the most remote villages and farmsteads of the Murgia will soon be affected by the change.

Figure 1
Apulia occupies a
central position in the
Mediterranean region.
Brindisi, its major port,
lies nearly equidistant
from Rome, Athens,
and Palermo. The
Adriatic Sea separates
Apulia from Yugo-
slavia by 120 miles and
from Albania by only
50 miles. The area of
the following map is
indicated by the dotted
outline.

Figure 2
Apulia. The heavy
dotted line is the
political boundary. The
area of the following
map is indicated by the
light dotted outline.

Figure 3
The Murgia of the
Trulli. The light area
indicates the top of the
Murgia, and the heavily
shaded areas, the
slopes at its edges.

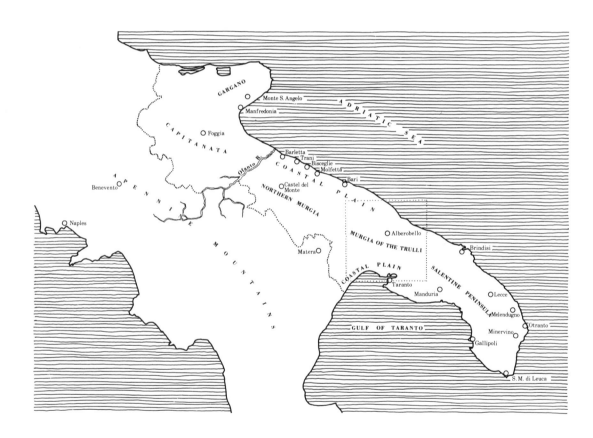

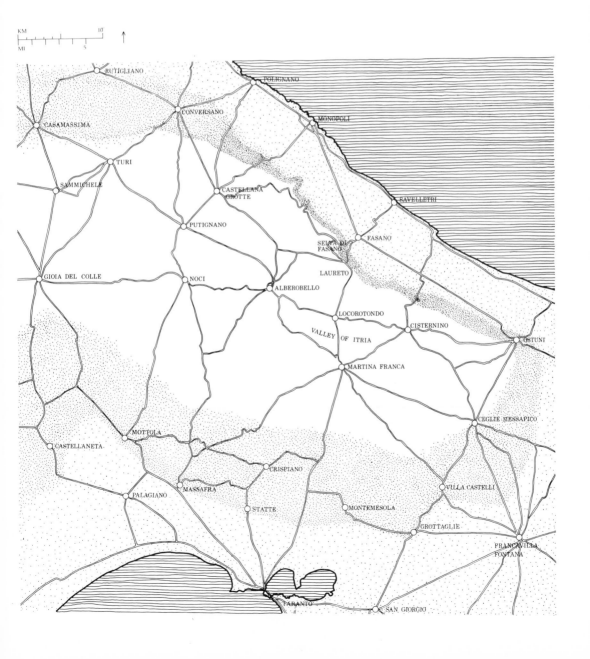

Figure 4
The northeastern flank of the Murgia of the Trulli rises steeply from the well-tended olive groves of the flat Adriatic plain between Fasano and Ostuni.

Figure 5
The soft, homogeneous *tufo* band of the southern edge of the Murgia is quarried for building blocks near Massafra. The black object in the center of the photograph is an upturned wheelbarrow.

Figure 6
A wall-lined road south
of Cisternino winds
through a typical
Murgia landscape.
Trullo domes can be
seen on the horizon
among the olive trees.

Figure 7
Limestone bedrock
projects from beneath
well-laid stone walls
on the Via del
Convento, near
Cisternino, on the
Murgia of the Trulli.

II

Of Wood and Stone

It is impossible to determine what type of shelter was the first to be constructed in Apulia. Archaeological studies have revealed remains of a number of different kinds of primitive shelters, some of which were apparently built contemporaneously, often in close proximity to one another. These include *capanne*, which were huts with wooden roof structures; caves, natural, manmade, or combinations of both; megalithic stone structures, including dolmens and menhirs; and microlithic stone structures such as the cairnlike *specchie* and corbelled-dome *trullo* shelters.

Remains of the wood-roofed *capanne* are found in many localities both on and off the Murgia. The remains of these huts consist of stone foundations and thick pieces of crude plaster made from *bolo* soil which bear the impressions of closely spaced wood poles that spanned the roof. Sometimes these huts were partially dug into the ground as a type of pit dwelling. In plan shape they varied from round to rectangular. The round plan was generally used in the earlier and more primitive dwellings. In some excavations of settlements occupied over long periods of time, successive superimposed layers of foundations exhibit a progression from circular plans in the lowest layers to ovals, rounded-corner rectangles, and finally rectangular plans in the upper strata. This same pattern of plan shape evolution has often been observed in other parts of the world.[1] Stone foundations unearthed in a number of Bronze Age communities discovered along ancient, long-dry river beds near Cisternino are circular in plan, having walls up to three feet thick and five feet high.[2]

The capital city of the Peucetians at Monte Sannace had public buildings and city walls of carefully worked blocks of *tufo*, but its houses were of wood. The mortared limestone foundations of these houses still remain, irregularly quadrilateral in plan, often with tombs of sacrificial babies beneath.[3] The roofs were apparently of semicylindrical burned clay tiles over a wooden structure.

Although the wooden houses at Monte Sannace may have been of fairly sophisticated manufacture, there is little evidence to suggest that wood construction ever reached a high degree of refinement in Apulia. The practice of building wooden roof structures for permanent habitations died out sufficiently long ago that scarcely any such structures remain today. In part this can be attributed to an early deforestation of timber suitable for construction, but it seems probable that once the techniques were learned, it was faster, less troublesome, and more permanent to build roof structures of the abundant stone. Stone-roofed houses offered the additional amenity of remaining refreshingly cool through the hottest days of the long summer.

Cave dwellings existed in abundance during neolithic times. The walls of the *gravine* of the Murgia offered a certain number of natural grottos which could be inhabited. Such grottos were often amplified by work with simple tools. As families or communities expanded, entirely new caves were sometimes dug alongside the seminatural ones. Neolithic cave dwellings and cave tombs have been discovered in the *tufo*-walled *gravina* at Matera, yielding pottery of a type made only on the Balkan Peninsula and apparently brought by traders. An entire neolithic community including both caves and *capanne* once thrived at Molfetta, north of Bari on the coastal plain, centering in and around the Pulo, an immense natural pit in the limestone bedrock, 550 feet long, 450 feet wide, and 115 feet deep. The *capanne* and a necropolis were on the plain above the pit, and the caves were dug from its walls. Traces of a road paved with stone blocks winds through the necropolis.[4]

Near Bisceglie, in a district several miles from the Pulo of Molfetta, a scattered group of dolmens are found alongside a deep ravine filled with ancient cave dwellings. The dolmens are almost certainly a product of the cave-and-*capanna*-dwelling society of the ravines and the Pulo. They did not serve as dwellings. A cave house could be easily chipped out with rudimentary tools by a man working alone, but a dolmen with its multiton slabs of stone could be made only by a concerted community effort, and invariably served as a burial place for an important man. In the vicinity of this ravine four dolmens are presently found, and a fifth of the same type is located on the coastal plain between Cisternino and the sea in another area with abundant remains of troglodytic shelters.[5]

In each of these five dolmens the burial chamber consists of three limestone slabs set on edge as walls, with a fourth slab resting horizontally across the top as a "roof." A gallery of upright slabs, perhaps originally roofed with wood, extends toward the east, and apparently once served as a chamber for the funerary banquet as well as for access to the burial chamber from outside a mound of earth and rock which covered the entire construction. The Dolmen of Bisceglie, best known of this group, yielded eight skeletons and numerous artifacts which date its construction at about 1200 to 1000 B.C., in the final Bronze Age. Land-clearing farmers had removed all but traces of the covering mound by the time of the archeological excavations, more than a half-century ago, and now only some of the stone slabs remain. The Dolmen of Albarosa, less than a mile farther up the same ravine, is still covered by a large rectangular rock pile, but the pile has been greatly deformed in relatively recent times to facilitate the construction of an adjacent *trullo* shelter. The Dolmen of San Silvestro has also suffered because of its incorporation into subsequent construction. The nearby Tavola dei Paladini dolmen had a well-preserved gallery early in this century, but presently only the burial chamber remains with its three walls and precariously perched capstone. At the time of the discovery of the Dolmen of Cisternino, in 1910, it had already long been in use as a field shelter, and its owner cheerfully confessed to having removed its superimposed mound thirty years before.[6] Traces of its gallery still remain, but the burial chamber has had its missing back wall carefully replaced by one made of mortared *tufo* blocks which has a little square window hole in it.

Another group of dolmens, quite different from the five just described, are found deep in the Salentine Peninsula. Sixteen of this type have been discovered in modern times, probably the survivors of a far greater number, but at last count only twelve were still in existence. Excavations in and around these dolmens have yielded nothing, so they cannot be dated. Unlike the group farther north, they do not have a set orientation and they do not have galleries. Their great capstones, rather than being supported by three upright wall-slabs, are held either by a number of smaller slabs or by numerous stacks of untrimmed stones. A fairly common feature is a hole through the center of the capstone, perhaps for pouring in drink offerings to the dead, which implies that the covering mounds probably came only to the level of the top of the dolmen, leaving the surface of the roof exposed. Some capstones have channels of unknown function carved around their edges. These Salentine dolmens as a group bear a strong resemblance to dolmens discovered on the islands of Malta and Sardinia.[7]

The Salentine dolmens, like those of the Bari region to the north, are suffering continuing destruction. Their mounds were long ago cleared away, probably in most cases the underlying dolmens with them, and the great stone slabs that were left are slowly disappearing. One authority, in 1914, noting sadly the then-recent destruction of a dolmen near the Dolmen of Scusi, concluded that the only dolmens which had survived the land-clearing zeal of the local farmers were those large enough to be useful as field shelters. The Dolmen of Quattro Macini was found inhabited by sheep.[8] The smaller Dolmen of Melendugno has been allowed to fall into a meaningless heap of rubble.

In the same two areas where dolmens occur, menhirs are found. These are much more numerous than the dolmens; about seventy still exist. Most are plain, squared billets of stone set solidly into sockets in the living rock and rising to heights up to fifteen feet. Some occur in more elaborate forms, such as the well-known anthropomorphic Monaco (monk) of Modugno, near Bari. The function of the menhirs is not known, although it is thought that they were idols for a cult of sun-worshippers. Such idolatry was not quickly replaced by Christianity, for church records beginning with the Council of Tours in 567 A.D. and continuing into the tenth century contain several references to the problem of menhir worship. The church's solutions seem to have been two: the carving on the menhirs of Latin crosses, many still in evidence today, and the uprooting of other menhirs for subsequent re-erection atop the roofs of Christian churches.

Like the dolmens, the menhirs have close counterparts in other regions of the Mediterranean. Among the most interesting are the numerous menhirs, many anthropomorphic, recently found on Corsica.[9]

The dolmens and menhirs were not shelters in the strict sense. The difficulty of organizing sufficient manpower and of finding large stone slabs in sufficient quantity and suitable sizes made megalithic techniques unfit for the erection of domestic shelters.

Two types of the microlithic *specchie* are found in Apulia. One includes small, flat, conical rock tumuli up to seven feet in height and thirty feet in diameter. These occur in slightly varying forms in groups throughout the Murgia of the Trulli. They are thought to be Peucetic in origin, and date from the Iron Age, sometime after 900 B.C. Each contains a dolmenic chamber housing a single crouched skeleton.[10] Though smaller in scale, they would seem precisely analogous to the dolmens with their covering mounds of stone and earth.

The *speechie* of the second type are much larger, zigguratlike piles of stone measuring up to fifty feet in height and seventy feet in diameter. No tombs or artifacts of any consequence have been found beneath them, although some have revealed during their demolition an underlying structure of large squared stones such as were used in the Messapian walls of the city of Manduria in the Salentine Peninsula. These *specchie* seem to have served as communications posts, watchtowers, and fortresses, for they are located within sight of one another, always on the highest points of land, on the southern end of the Murgia in what was once the border area between Messapia and Peucetia. A chain of these gigantic unmortared towers once guarded the Salentine Peninsula from the Gulf of Taranto to the Adriatic. They were joined by a wall, called Il Paretone, also of mortarless stonework about ten feet in thickness at the base and probably once at least equal to that in height.[11]

These great defense and communications *specchie* have been tentatively assigned to the Iron Age, the same as the smaller burial *specchie* with the dolmenic chambers.[12] About 140 of them still exist, with the greatest concentration in the district surrounding Ceglie Messapico and Francavilla Fontana, but the extent to which the existing *specchie* have been quarried for construction gives ample grounds for speculation on how many more there may once have been. Most segments of the immense Paretone have disappeared.

Around some of the large *specchie* have been discovered the ruins of ancient villages of *trullo* shelters. These communities of corbelled-dome huts apparently housed the troops which manned the *specchie*. It is possible that every large *specchia* once had its supporting village, but that agricultural land clearing has removed the traces of many.[13]

The exact origin of the *trullo* form of construction in Apulia is the subject of much scholarly dispute. As shelters that are structurally similar have been found in areas such as Egypt, Mesopotamia, Greece,

Dalmatia, Sicily, and Sardinia, the concept could easily have been imported. The earliest vaulting erected by the Egyptians and the Mesopotamians, in the third millenium B.C., was of the *trullo* type. The tholos form of Greece is well known, and its Greek spelling τρουλλoζ lends some etymological support to a theory of importation from that country. The *nuraghi* of Sardinia, several thousands of which still exist, are large, curious constructions resembling a cross between the *specchia* and the Salentine *chipuro*. Their siting, artifacts, and construction all suggest that their purpose was defense. At ground level each contains a fair-sized chamber vaulted in *trullo* fashion, from the entry of which a stone stairway built within the wall winds up to one or two upper levels. Some are more than thirty feet in diameter.[14] The similarity of Sardinian and Salentine dolmens, together with the resemblance of the *nuraghi* to the *specchie* and the *chipuri*, suggests strongly that some sort of linkage existed between the two cultures.

There is a theory which holds that the *trullo* form was used first for tombs or for fortifications, and later was adapted for domestic use.[15] Remains have yet to be found in Apulia which would support these arguments, although in Greece tholos tombs were built, and in Sardinia the defensive *nuraghi* were vaulted *trullo*-fashion.

It is possible that the technique could have been invented in Apulia independently of other areas of the world. Small children playing with flat stones on the beach have been observed to spontaneously build *trullo* forms.[16] The author once saw New England school children constructing a large play igloo *trullo*-fashion from thick, flat crusts of dry snow. *Trullo* structures occur in virtually every part of the world where suitable stone is available, and stop where the stone disappears. In any of these areas, a farmer clearing his fields for cultivation would have been as likely as not to discover the technique for himself.

Very old *trullo* shelters are hard to find. The structures had to be closely fitted together in a planned sequence from bottom to top, and damage to the middle of the construction could be very difficult to repair. In most cases it was simpler and safer to tear down and rebuild the entire shelter, taking advantage of the occasion to incorporate the latest innovations from one's neighbor's house. The oldest *trullo* shelters still in existence are said to date from a time no earlier than the sixteenth century.[17] Nevertheless, one can still occasionally find on the Murgia a structure with thick, low walls, a round floor plan, and no openings except for a low doorway, a *trullo* shelter of a more primitive type. As the technique developed the walls became thinner and taller, and as in the case of the *capanne*, the shape of the interior space became rectangular. Smoke holes, chimneys, fireplaces, alcoves, and windows were all relatively late innovations in this method of construction, as was the practice of joining together two or more domes to form a more complex set of spaces.

Trullo shelters occur in four distinct and separate areas of Apulia: the Salentine Peninsula, in the same areas as the dolmens and menhirs; the Murgia of the Trulli; the coastal plain around and to the north of Bari (where they stand by the thousands in close proximity to the dolmens and caves), and including part of the Northern Murgia around Castel del Monte; and near Monte Sant'Angelo in the mountains of Gargano. The gaps among these four areas can be explained by the discontinuity of the occurrence of suitable stone. Only on the Murgia of the Trulli are *trullo* shelters widely used for permanent occupancy. In the other three areas they serve as agricultural day shelters, toolsheds, or huts for occupancy during harvest time. The well-developed corbelled stone shelters of the Murgia are the only ones correctly called *trulli*. The other *trullo* forms of Apulia go by other names: *caselle* or *casedde* along the coastal plain, and *chipuri*, derived from the Greek word meaning "guardians of the field," on the Salentine Peninsula.[18] The word *trullo* is used only in educated Italian. *Trudd*, *truddu*, and *truddo* are dialect forms of the name commonly heard on the Murgia.

Of the primitive shelters of Apulia, the dolmens, menhirs, and *specchie*, religious and military in purpose, became obsolete sometime during the Greek and Roman occupations, and are seen today only as lifeless ruins. *Capanne* are still used for field shelters in an area near Conversano, where they are called *pagghiari*, and are built today in a somewhat different form on the Adriatic coast just below Gargano, but have never been developed extensively as permanent habitations. The caves and *trullo* shelters, by contrast, proved practical as permanent shelters and continued to develop slowly through the centuries.

In the centuries after the Greek and Roman occupations, the pace of development changed. Religious persecution in the Byzantine Empire caused the cave shelter to be brought to a high plane of architectural refinement within a few decades. The taxation policies of the king of Naples and the ambitions of a petty feudal baron combined to rapidly push the capabilities of the once-crude *trullo* shelter to new heights. And the continuing conflicts of troubled times made a newer, imported technique, mortared stone vaulting, the only economical system for the construction of the hill towns of the Murgia. In these three forms, caves, *trulli*, and vaulted stone, the stone shelters of the Murgia of the Trulli achieved maturity.

Figures 2 and 3
A *pagghiaro*, one of a small number still standing between Conversano and Rutigliano, serves as a field shelter. Its roof structure consists of trimmed tree branches, grapevine prunings, and a straw covering. These few huts are virtually the only remaining shelters in the area of the Murgia of the Trulli that use wood as a primary structural material, and are the closest extant approximation of *capanne* in Apulia.

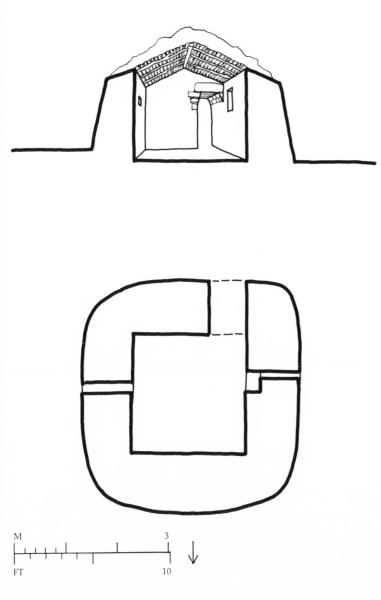

M

FT

3

10

Figure 4
The Dolmen of
Bisceglie is the best
preserved of the gallery
graves in the area
around Bari. The
remnants of the
upright gallery slabs
can be seen in the
lower right-hand
corner of the photo-
graph, leading away
from the burial
chamber.

Figure 5
The Tavola dei
Paladini is the burial
chamber of another
gallery grave in the
same area as the
Dolmen of Bisceglie.

Following pages
Figure 6
The Dolmen Placa,
near Melendugno in the
Salentine Peninsula.

Figure 7
The Dolmen of Scusi,
near Minervino di
Lecce, has a large hole
bored through the
center of its massive
eighteen-inch-thick
capstone.

Figure 8
The low Dolmen of
Quattro Macini
exhibits both a hole
through its capstone
and a channel carved
around its edge.

Figure 9
Plans of five dolmens
drawn to the same
scale. The first three
are northern Apulian
gallery graves: (a) the
Tavola dei Paladini;
(b) the Dolmen of
Bisceglie; (c) the
Dolmen of Cisterino.
The last two are
Salentine dolmens: (d)
the Dolmen Placa; (e)
the Dolmen of Scusi.
The orientations shown
on the drawing do not
relate to the actual
orientations of these
structures.

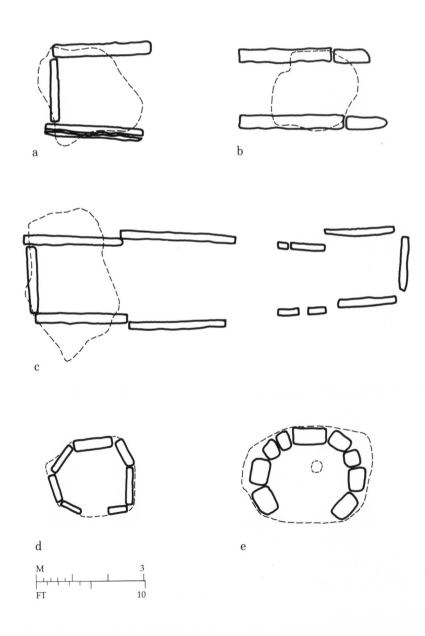

Figure 10
Not far from the
Dolmen of Quattro
Macini, a menhir juts
ten feet skyward from
a rock outcrop at an
ancient crossroads.

Figure 11
The Specchia Miano
crowns a hilltop
between Francavilla
Fontana and Ceglie
Messapico. It is
roughly thirty-five
feet high and sixty-five
feet in diameter. It has
six concentric stone
terraces and a small,
square roofless room
with a doorway at its
topmost level.

Figure 12
South of Cisternino, in
the vicinity of the half-
ruined Specchia
Sativa, can be found a
considerable stretch of
the Paretone, the great
stone wall which once
divided Messapia from
Peucetia. It probably
stood ten or more feet
tall, more than twice
its present height.

Figure 13
Areas of occurrence of
trullo shelters in
Apulia.

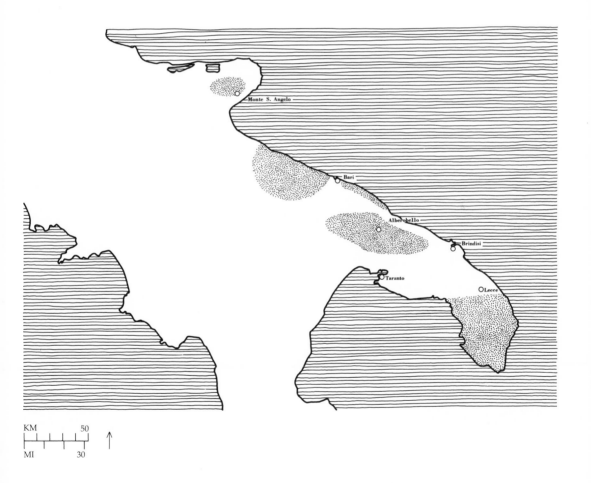

KM   50
MI   30

Figures 14 and 15
A crudely built
shepherd's hut on the
Gargano Massif is
spanned *trullo* fashion.
The door lintel is a
particularly interest-
ing construction. A
stone-walled corral or
shed, now in ruins, is
attached by the
doorway. The
unfinished vault is
spanned by sticks of
wood and a covering
of sod. The floor is of
earth.

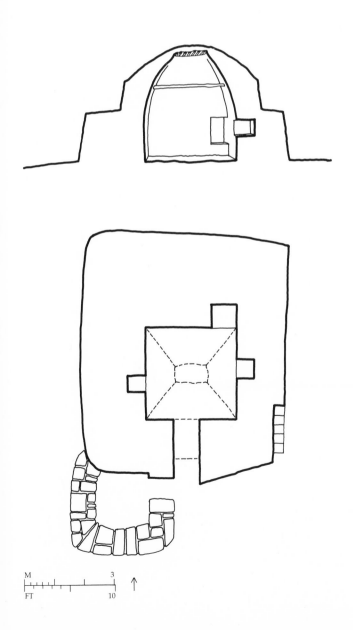

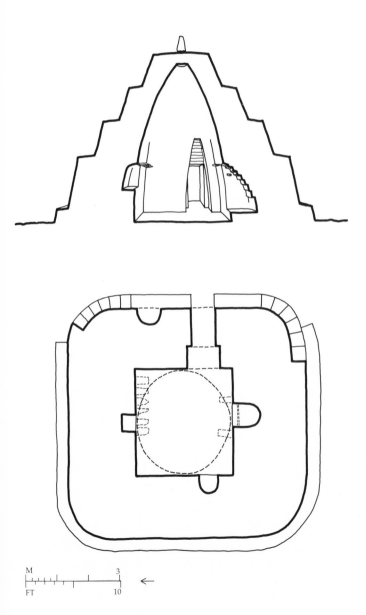

Figures 16 and 17
A typical *casella* of
the coastal area north
of Bari is roofed in
concentric terraces.
Outside stairs allow
these terraces to be
used for the drying of
produce. The four
niches, one exterior
and three interior, are
spanned with corbels.
The exterior door
lintel is of stone slabs,
and the interior of the
doorway opening is
corbelled. Projecting
flat stones form
interior shelves.

M   3
|+++++|+++|+| | ←
FT   10

Figures 18 and 19
A small concentration
of *trullo* shelters occurs
near the Castel del
Monte on the Northern
Murgia. This simple
example has a dirt
floor and a unique
half-vault over the
entry space.

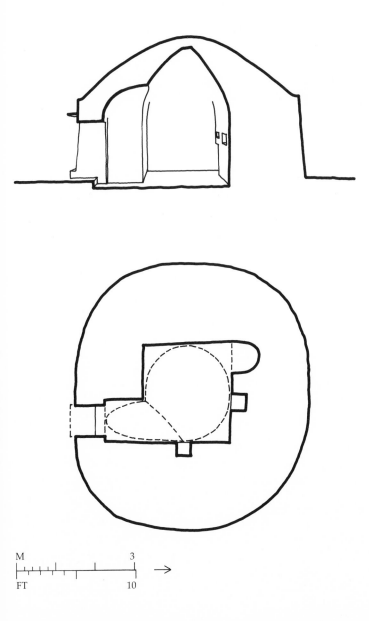

M
3
FT
10

Figure 20
The more elaborate
shelters at Castel del
Monte have stone
floors and a unique
structure utilizing
carefully constructed
arches of *tufo* blocks
as primary elements of
support. This
particular shelter has
an exterior cistern.

Figure 21
Stone devices used for
spanning doorways in
chipuri. No scale.

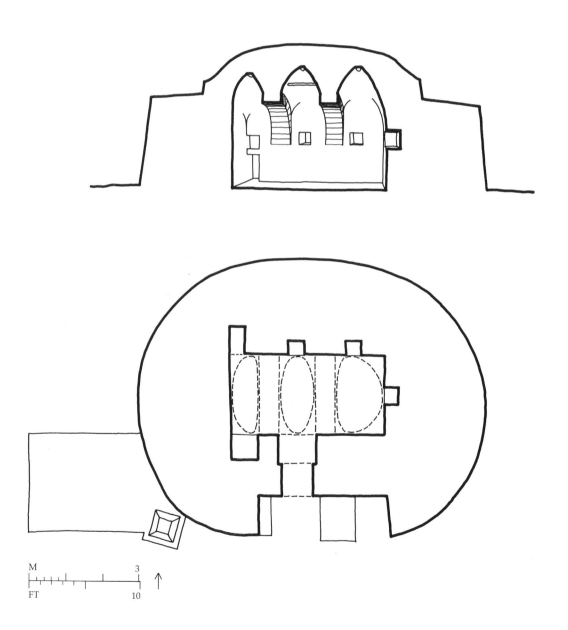

M ⊢┼┼┼┼─┼───┤ 3
FT   10

Figures 22 and 23
Shelters of the Salentine Peninsula are most often made in a truncated cone shape with a gently rounded sod roof. This *chipuro* is round in plan both inside and out, and has a small window opening.

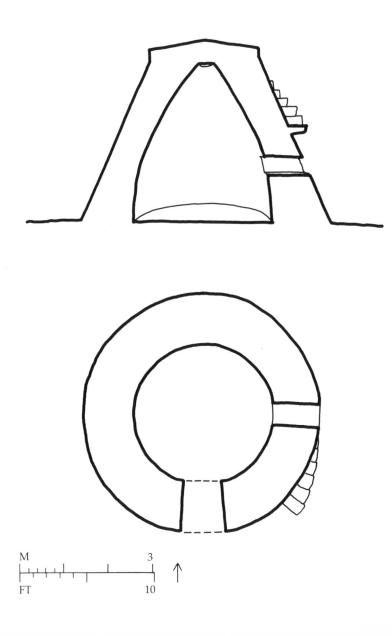

M ⊢ 3 ↑
FT 10

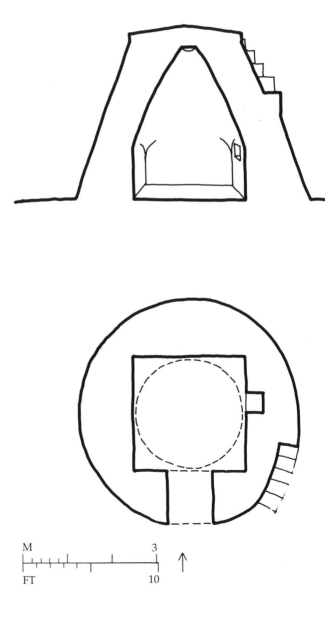

M   3

FT   10

Figures 24 and 25
This *chipuro* is square
in its internal plan,
though still round
outside.

Figures 26 and 27
A beautifully
constructed Salentine
chipuro of square plan.

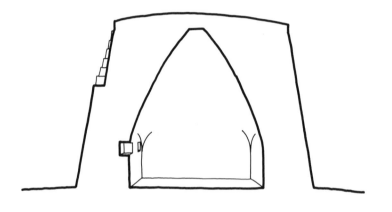

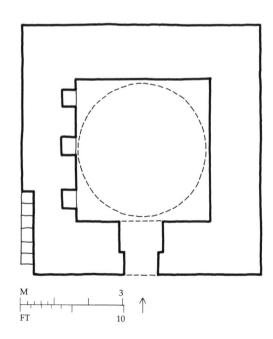

M   3

FT   10

III

From Solid Stone: Massafra

Every deep-scored *gravina* of the soft southern edge of the Murgia of the Trulli once had its yielding *tufo* walls tunneled out as shelter for a cave community. Matera, Ginosa, Laterza, Castellaneta, Palagianello, Mottola, Massafra, Crispiano, Montemesola, Grottaglie—each modern town has near it one or five or a dozen such canyons, now wild and desolate, populated by scurrying lizards, circling birds, and tangled undergrowth, but lined with cliffs still honeycombed by the many levels of dusty chambers and empty passages of long-abandoned villages. One such village thrived for a time in the Gravina of the Madonna della Scala at Massafra.

This village is said to date from Messapian times. According to one account Messapo, brother of Tara, built a fortified village of two hundred families on the site of the present-day town of Massafra, on a point of land above the mouth of the *gravina*, in the year 754 B.C. He named it Messapha. After being troubled by earthquakes and skirmishes with neighboring peoples, the inhabitants of Messapha moved to the coastal plain, only to be plagued there with floods and malaria. On their eventual return to the edge of the Murgia, one part of the population took up residence in caves which they excavated in the *gravina*, whereas the other part dug communal cave dwellings called *vicinanze* (literally *neighborhoods*) from the plain above. In time the original city of Messapha was repopulated and became an outpost of the Greek colony at Taranto.[1]

The cave town as it exists today is largely the product of developmental activity which began in the *gravina* in the sixth century A.D., with the first of the Greco-Byzantine Immigrations.[2] It was then, hard on the heels of the conquering Byzantine armies, that Basilian monks first came to Apulia and founded their cliff-monasteries. The most intensive development of the town took place during the period 717–843 A.D., when the iconoclasts were in power in Byzantium. Under Leo III, the first iconoclast, sixty thousand monks fled to exile in Italy rather than break their vows, and brought with them their skills as painters of icons.[3] Every *gravina* was soon occupied by the boatloads of refugees who trekked up the slopes from the harbor at Taranto, and a chain of dozens of troglodytic communities stretched from Matera to Grottaglie, a distance of fifty miles.

The golden age of the settlement in the Gravina of the Madonna della Scala lasted from the eighth through the eleventh centuries. The population, monastic and secular, of all the caves around Massafra grew to an estimated two thousand. Local farmers found the monastery a source of knowledge about agricultural problems and a center for the dispensation of healing herbs and medicines. Greek became the spoken language, and Eastern Orthodoxy became the prevailing religion.[4]

Beginning in the eleventh century, during the last stand of the Byzantines against the Normans in Apulia, the low-lying, indefensible cave towns were gradually abandoned in favor of fortified communities on higher ground. Under the Roman Catholic conquerors, the Byzantine monks and their followers were subjected to considerable pressure to change their allegiance. Despite this pressure, diminishing remnants of the monks survived into the seventeenth century, when the last of the icons were painted on the walls of the cave churches.[5]

The Gravina of the Madonna della Scala is about three miles long. The cave village, only a quarter of a mile in length, is located less than a mile from the mouth of the *gravina*. The northwestern cliff was apparently devoted to private dwellings, shops, and stables. The southeastern cliff was given almost entirely to monastic and public uses. At its northern end is a gigantic natural arch now called the Grotto of Cyclops. The size of this sheltered space suggests that it may have served as a forum for the community, for its market, public gatherings, and religious ceremonies. The bottom of the *gravina* was the main axis of circulation, connecting with steep stairs and slanting paths, liberally provided with handholds, leading to the various levels of shelters. The paths may also have assisted in collecting rainwater as it coursed down the steep cliffs, and in diverting it into cisterns for the use of the citizenry. Sewage was probably carried up the cliffs to be spread over the fields above as fertilizer. Two crypt churches were dug at the southern end of the southeastern cliff. The older of the two, dating from the eighth or ninth century, is relatively crude in form and completely devoid of decoration except for Latin crosses of doubtful origin which are scratched on its walls. The newer church, just above, was more formal in plan and execution, and was covered inside with frescoes in the twelfth or thirteenth century, after the Gravina had been largely abandoned. Most of this chapel was destroyed by the Ingegner Scarcia of Taranto to make way for his undistinguished eighteenth-century church of the Madonna della Scala.[6]

High on the cliff above the Grotto of Cyclops is a remarkable set of chambers known as the Pharmacy of Mago Greguro. In these linked rooms, all on about the same level, one can still see traces of a cistern, canals, settling basins, and drying benches, all carved in the rock, used for the production of medicines from herbs. In several walls hundreds of carved niches in regular patterns served to hold the jars of finished medicines. A recent botanical survey of the *gravina* established that more than 250 varieties of medicinal herbs still grow wild in the vicinity of the Pharmacy.[7]

The hundreds of cave houses in the northwestern cliff vary greatly in detail, but have many common characteristics. The elementary house is a single fan-shaped room with its door at the narrow end. Both ceiling and floor are flat. An alcove may be attached for storage or sleeping. Some houses have beautifully detailed fireplaces carved into the walls, with chimneys exiting through the steep slope above. Doors, windows, and chimney openings are protected from rainwater running down the surface of the cliff by carefully chiseled drainage channels. Cylindrical storage chambers or cisterns below floor level may have served for the keeping of water, wine, or grain. Frequent rope attachments fashioned from the *tufo* ceilings probably held bunches of drying herbs or braided chains of fruit or vegetables. Oil lamps shone from niches in the walls; larger niches held household items or furnished counter space. The entrance doorways, reached from outside by carved stairways, were probably closed by woven mats or animal hides. There is no evidence to suggest that these caves were ever whitewashed or painted either outside or in.

The workmanship evidenced in the caves is generally good. Careful chisel work was used in the manufacture of the drip channels above the openings, the detailing of many door frames, the finishing of the fireplaces and chimneys, and the working of the flanged openings in the subfloor storage chambers. The rounded wall-ceiling junctions and the visible tool marks in many spaces suggest that the major part of the excavation was done with a narrow-bladed metal adze. A few days must have sufficed to create an average-sized dwelling by this method. The later crypt churches such as the newer chapel in the Gravina of the Madonna della Scala, or the churches in the adjacent Gravina San Marco, are of particularly fine manufacture, with their surfaces carefully planed and their corners well finished. Their not-quite-rectangular plans may have resulted from the difficulties involved in laying out a perfectly square construction when carving space from a solid medium, or perhaps from the fact that in conventional buildings accuracy of layout is essential only to make the building go together more easily and not for the smooth functioning of the finished product. There was no compelling reason why a cave church had to be perfectly square.

The reasons for the basic shape given to the cave dwellings by their makers are an interesting matter for speculation. In theory, virtually any shape of space could have been easily hacked from this yielding, homogeneous substance. Why then did the cave builders choose to make fan-shaped rooms with flat ceilings, when the builders of the *capanne* and *trullo* shelters were making the progression from round floor plans to rectangular ones?

The fan-shaped plan seems to have offered several advantages to its builder-occupants. It was a convenient way to dig a cave, working through a single opening and branching off from it radially, pushing the rapidly accumulating debris back through the doorway. The finished room, with two straight walls, square corners, and a gently curving back wall, was in plan a bent rectangle which offered most of the advantages of rectangularity while doing away with one of its frequent problems, dark corners. The simple cave dwelling is evenly illuminated from its single opening. The back wall is at all points approximately equidistant from the opening, and the dark door-wall is kept relatively short. The larger cave complex is generally a connected series of fan-shapes, each room provided with an appropriate door or windows for its illumination and ventilation.

The flat ceilings, requiring the removal of the least rock, were permitted by the fact that the *tufo*, although structurally a very weak material, could flat-span quite large rooms because of its great depth. Occasionally a caved-in ceiling shows that the structural limitations of the *tufo* were exceeded, but generally plenty of depth was left between the ceiling of a cave and the floor of the one above. The cave churches sometimes have arched openings, arcaded aisles, and domed ceilings, but these are stylistic devices and were not structurally necessary.

One of the few technical problems encountered by the cave digger was how to know as he chopped his way through the stone when he was approaching too closely his neighbor's cave or another con- volution of the surface of the cliff. The ragged shapes and inexplicable locations of many windows and inter-cave openings in the otherwise well-tailored grottos are evidence that miscalculations were fre- quent. Further evidence is furnished by the numerous caves whose entire front faces have sheared off their too-thin supports and slid to the bottom of the *gravina*.

Tufo is a marvelous material. It is dense enough and hard enough to have served as both exterior and interior finishes, yet soft and fine-grained enough to have been cut into almost any shape for any pur- pose. Because of the immense height, length, and thickness of the *tufo* cliffs, great freedom of planning was possible. A simple cave could be enlarged, changed in shape, have another chamber added to it behind, to one side, above or below, linked by ramp, stair, or doorway, and then another chamber beyond that, and yet another, perhaps in a different direction, or branching off from one of the new chambers. Built-in furnishings more often saved labor than caused labor, for they represented material that did not have to be loosened and hauled away.

Yet the freedom was not total. The cliff could be pierced and hollowed out, but it could not be added to without the laborious importation of outside materials, especially mortar. Moreover, one could not burrow too deeply away from the face, because only at the face were sunlight and air available.

The only fatal weakness of the cave system of shelter in Byzantine times was its indefensibility. The cave city in the great *gravina* at Matera, which could be defended, has been populated continuously since before the beginning of recorded history. Later, under the pressure of a population which at one time approached thirty thousand, the spatial capacity of its cliff face became overtaxed. Mortared stone vaulting was used to extend the crowded cave houses into the free air, and additional chambers were dug far back into the *tufo*. Healthful standards of light, air, and sanitation could no longer be maintained. Presently its inhabitants, many unwillingly, are being moved to new, faceless apartment buildings on the plain above, and their cave houses blocked so they cannot go back.

The making of a cave is the antithesis of the usual construction process. A cave is space produced directly by the subtraction of a relatively small amount of solid material from a very large mass. A more conventional shelter, whether it be a *trullo*, a vaulted stone townhouse, or the reader's own dwelling, is space produced indirectly by its enclosure with pieces of solid material added together. It is interesting to speculate what shape Manhattan Island might have taken if it would have had a deep covering of *tufo* when bought from the Indians, especially considering that according to Thoreau's account, many of New York's early Dutch settlers built and occupied pit dwellings before they were able to afford above-ground accommodations.[8]

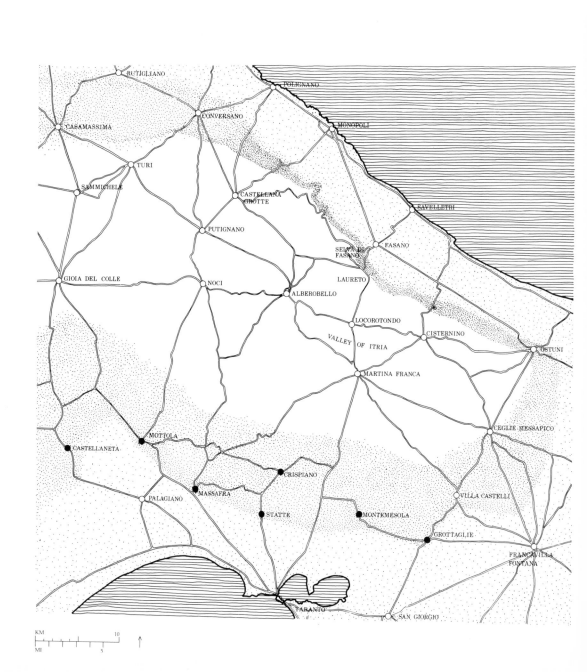

KM   10

MI   5

Figure 1
The cave towns of the
Murgia of the Trulli are
located in the *gravine*
between Matera and
Grottaglie, near the
modern towns indicated
on the map.

Figure 2
A sketch map of the
Gravina of the
Madonna della Scala
of Massafra. The
northwestern cliff was
devoted to secular
uses, and the south-
eastern cliff to two
churches, a monastery,
a pharmacy, and a large
grotto which may have
served for public
gatherings. The date of
the large retaining walls
near the pharmacy is
not known; possibly
they were built in
Byzantine times to
enlarge and improve
the space available
outside the grotto. The
representation of cave
openings is schematic
only, and is intended to
indicate the relative
concentrations of caves
in various locations.

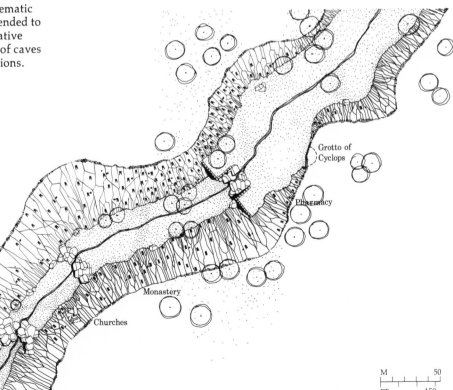

Grotto of
Cyclops

Pharmacy

Monastery

Churches

M 50
FT 150

Figure 3
The northwestern cliff
displays the ruins of
many cave houses. In
some cases the cliff face
has fallen away to
expose the interior
spaces. The stone
retaining walls are of
recent construction.

Figure 4
The southeastern cliff
contains the Grotto of
Cyclops, center, and the
Pharmacy of Mago
Greguro, the chain of
openings high in the
cliff to the right. This
area has suffered
extensive damage from
rockfalls. Beyond the
edge of the photograph
to the right are the
monastery and the cave
churches.

Figure 5
Many chimney openings, some with carved rain gutters above, are evident in this photograph of a group of cave dwellings. Four doorways can be seen. The large rock mass in the center foreground has fallen from the cliff above.

Figure 6
This two-story corner of the monastery has been opened by a major rockfall which has removed both the outside wall and a large portion of the floor.

Figure 7
A low doorway with two steps connects two rooms of the monastery. At the lower right is a flanged opening into a subfloor storage chamber.

Figure 8
A similar doorway opens through a thin, pilastered wall into the lower room shown in Fig. 6. Note the clear tool marks in the right-hand corner of the room.

Figure 9
Three large niches are
carved into the outer
wall of this monastery
room.

Figure 10
Another view of the
same room shows its
connection to a room
beyond.

Figure 11
A crudely carved post
supports the flat ceiling
of the earlier cave
church in the Gravina
of the Madonna della
Scala. The workman-
ship and layout are not
as refined here as in the
remains of the later
cave church nearby.

Figure 12
The earlier cave church.
Two chimneys occur
along the outside wall.
A third post which once
supported the ceiling in
the center of the cave
has disappeared.

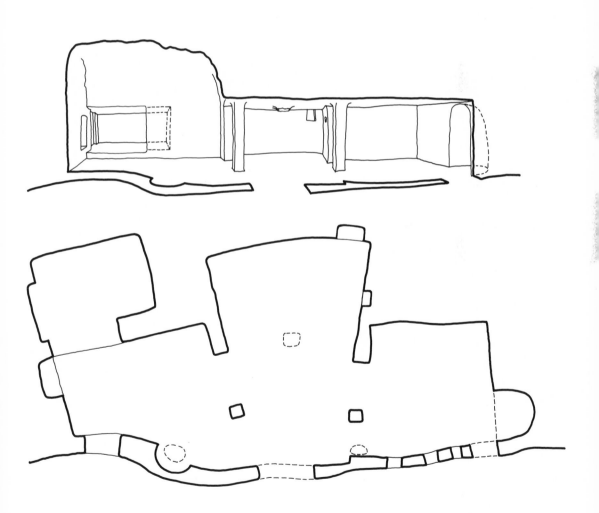

Figure 13
This cave shelter is of the simplest type, without window or chimney. Two wall niches are its only accessories.

Figure 14
This more elaborate house boasts two niches, an underfloor storage chamber, and a hooded fireplace with a dampered chimney. A carved stairway leads from its door toward the bottom of the *gravina*. The interior space is subdivided by two short spur walls.

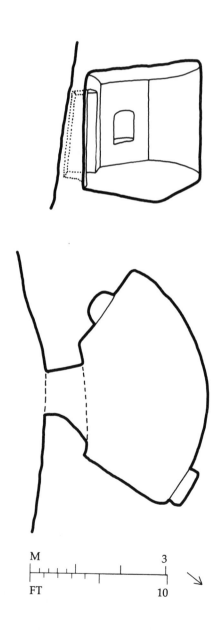

M   3

FT   10

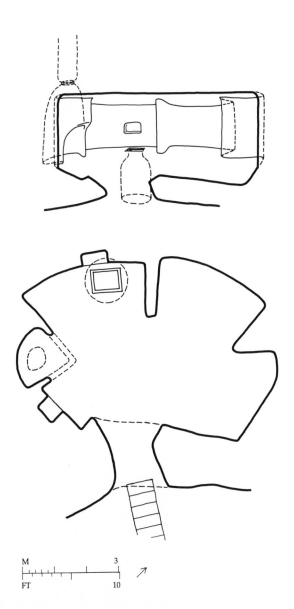

M
FT

Figure 15
This cave shelter, possibly a workshop-dwelling combination, occupies three levels. The lowest level, the hypothetical workshop, is reached from below by an outside stair. A carved ladder and a crawlway lead to the intermediate level, the dwelling, which is equipped with a fireplace. The small upper room might have served either for sleeping or for storage.

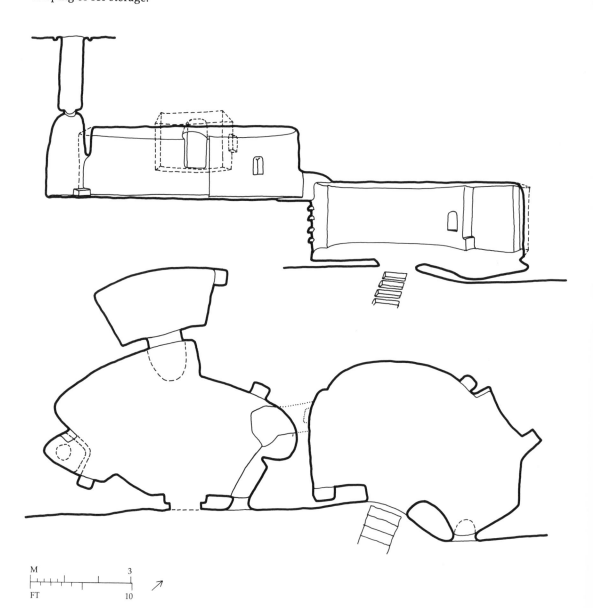

M ⊢┼┼┼┼┼──────┼──────┤ 3
FT   10

Figure 16
A sketch plan of the
Pharmacy of Mago
Greguro, taken from a
drawing by F. Morea in
Jacovelli's *S. Maria
della Scala di Massafra.*
Although not shown
here, the first three
chambers from the left
contain hundreds of
wall niches arranged in
regular rows.

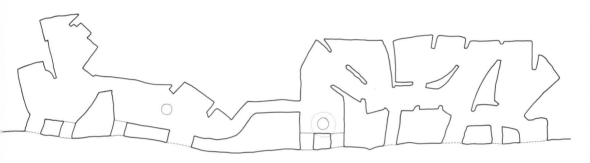

Figure 17

The monastery was built on five main levels, one over the other. The lowest level, partly obstructed by rockfalls and the gradual filling of the *gravina*, now has only two rooms open, one with a chimney and underfloor storage chamber. Small crosses on the plan indicate rope attachments carved into the ceiling. The second level is the most elaborate. Its first four rooms, their front wall missing, have a small oratory (b) with a central column and two flanking arches, and an altar-like counter (c) with a shallow cup and channel, perhaps for liturgical use or for processing herbs. Two other such counters are found on this floor, along with numerous rope attachments. On the cliff face at the extreme right is the start of a long, steep, angling stairway (d) to the upper levels. The third level, actually several interconnected levels, marks the beginning of two additional stairways: one outside, between the first and second floors from the left, leading directly to the fifth level (e); and the other inside, leading from the far right-hand room to the fourth level (f). This inside stair was probably supplemented by a wooden stair or ladder, for it begins several feet above floor level. The fourth level, in part reconstructed in this plan, has a subfloor storage chamber by the inside stairway. The floor of the interior room has curious channels of unknown use. A tiny carved ladder (g) leads from this level to the fifth.

Figure 18
These cave dwellings in
the town of Massafra
are still inhabited.
Unlike the houses of
the nearby Gravina of
the Madonna della
Scala, these have been
augmented with *tufo*
block construction and
have been white-
washed.

Figures 19 and 20
Two details of
contemporary Massafra
cave dwellings.

IV

Of Dry Stone: Alberobello

The first count of Conversano was given his lands and title in the Norman epoch, perhaps as a reward for services in the Crusades. His original fief lay just off the Murgia to the north. In July of 1480, one of his successors, Count Giulio Antonio I Acquaviva, was asked by the Aragonese king of Naples to gather an army and repel an imminent invasion of the Turks at Otranto. The count courageously and success-fully led his soldiers in this mission, but in the very moment of his victory he was unhorsed and killed. Nevertheless, the Turks had been successfully driven back into the sea, and although later in the same year they achieved a foothold in a subsequent invasion, the family of the count was rewarded for his services with further noble titles and with feudal rights to an adjacent, largely unpopulated piece of the Murgia of the Trulli which touched at its southwestern border the present-day towns of Noci, Putig-nano, and Martina Franca. Giulio's son and successor, Count Andrea Matteo, named this new territory Silva aut Nemus Arborbelli and began colonizing it with settlers from other parts of his realm, offering them free grants of land. By the year 1525, he had persuaded about forty families to settle in various parts of his new territory. When he lost interest in this venture later in life, he passed it on to his brother Giannantonio, who continued its development. By the mid-sixteenth century, under Giannan-tonio's control, farmers migrating from surrounding depressed areas had made a relatively dense settle-ment on the site which is now occupied by the Rione Monti of Alberobello. An estimate of the popula-tion of this one settlement, called the Selva, for the year 1616, a half-century later, was about forty families or two hundred people.[1]

In 1620, Gian Girolamo II, Duke of Nardò, who was called "the One-Eyed of Apulia" for his most prominent physical defect, inherited the title of count from his father, Giulio II. In 1635 he took steps to encourage the further growth of the Selva, constructing there a tavern, a delicatessen, a mill, a public oven, and a butcher shop. He offered to prospective immigrants inducements of unprecedented gener-osity, including long-term leases, direct financial aid, extension of credit, and immunity to criminals for crimes committed outside the Selva. Between 1635 and 1650 the population of the Selva, under these conditions, increased from about seventy families to over one hundred. Settlers came from as far away as the opposite shore of the Adriatic.[2]

The surrounding countryside also became more densely populated under his rule. Gian Girolamo, concerned with the rise of banditry along the country roads, offered special concessions to those who would live on their land, thus hoping to eventually populate the rural districts in sufficient density to eliminate the hiding places of the outlaws. In this attempt he was largely successful, for even today this is one of the few areas of Italy in which farmers live on their land rather than in villages. The idea, however, was not a new one. It had been successfully tried two centuries earlier by Philip I of Anjou, Prince of Taranto, in the vicinity of neighboring Martina Franca.[3]

For the settler in the Selva all was not happiness and prosperity, however. Gian Girolamo was a crude, violent, and ambitious man, and wished to develop the Selva as his own private monarchy independently of the Neapolitan king. To this end he kept his subjects virtually as prisoners. They had no legal rights whatsoever. The count exercised control through his private army by means of beatings, torture, and death.[4]

Gian Girolamo became an important force in the shaping of the stone shelters of the Murgia because of an edict known as the Prammatica de Baronibus which was sent by the Spanish king to all his barons, including the count of Conversano. The edict required royal permission for the construction of any new building. The intent of the law was to ensure that each baron would send to the king's treasury each year his just share of taxes, in proportion to the number and value of the buildings in his territory.[5] Gian Girolamo II, not wishing to divide his revenue with the king, nor to disclose the existence of his own rapidly developing monarchy, had no intention of reporting its developmental activity. On the other hand, he had to consider the possibility of an unpreventable on-site inspection by royal assessors.

If, the count reasoned, he required all new buildings to be built of stone, but without the use of mortar, the townspeople could certainly house themselves adequately in *trullo* shelters and at the first news of the approach of a royal assessor, the entire village could be quickly reduced to innocuous piles of stone such as existed in fields all over the Murgia. Reconstruction could be quickly accomplished by the villagers after the departure of the inspector.[6]

The count's reasoning was sound. In 1644, following some years of a mild boom in the construction of new *trullo* shelters, Francesco I Caracciolo, the duke of Martina Franca, became jealous of Gian Girolamo's successful evasion of taxes on his development at the Selva and brought charges against him in the royal court of Splain. Gian Girolamo heard of the subsequent approach of the king's investigator, and his forces in one activity-filled night ensured that only the houses previously known to the crown remained to be revealed by the dawn. The inspector arrived, found nothing out of order, and departed. The Selva was rebuilt from the same stones, again without mortar.[7]

The enemies of the count eventually had their revenge. In 1649 he was finally called to the court of King Philip IV of Spain to answer for his misdeeds, and he was subsequently kept in exile in Spain. In time he won again, through influential friends, the favor of the king, and was in the early stages of his return journey to Apulia in the spring of 1665 when, at Barcelona, he died.[8]

Through his successors, however, the hard-fisted policies of Gian Girolamo the One-Eyed lived on. But the population of the Selva nevertheless continued to increase. The Selva and the countryside around it continued to develop physically as well, still with houses of unmortared stone whose construction became increasingly refined with the passing of the generations.

Both the *trullo*, as it now came to be known, and the town of *trulli* called the Selva enjoyed their greatest development in the eighteenth century. As the end of the century approached, the Selva had a population estimated to have been as high as 3,500 and still growing. The current count of Conversano, Giulio Antonio Acquaviva, seemed firmly in control. But four priests, two doctors, and a master builder met clandestinely in the Selva to formulate a plan for gaining political freedom.[9]

May 9, 1797, found Ferdinand IV, the Bourbon king of Naples, arriving in Taranto to attend the wedding of his son Francesco I. But this was only half his mission; he also wished to tour this far corner of his kingdom in an effort to calm and consolidate it in the disturbing wake of the revolution in France. Two days later, on the recommendation of the wealthy cavalier Galeota of Taranto, he found himself confronted with the seven *selvesi*, who had traveled secretly by night to Taranto to plead for political independence for the Selva. They cited the abuses of the count against both them and the crown. The king seemed favorably disposed toward the plaintiffs, and promised to make an early decision on the matter. But, when after two weeks no word had come from the king, the *selvesi* were obliged to again intercept him in his journey, this time at Foggia, to the north, to ask for his verdict. After two days more of agonizing delay, the Selva was at last declared free and independent, a sovereign city responsible only to the king, on May 27, 1797.[10]

Less than a month later, the first council of the new city was held under a tree flanking the church. The primary business of the meeting was to choose a fitting name for this new political entity. The first proposal, "Ferdinandina," in honor of the liberating king, was passed over, and the name "Alberobello" adopted, meaning "Beautiful Tree," a corruption of *Arboris belli*, part of the Latin name given the area by Count Andrea Matteo three centuries before.[11]

The same year, with great celebration, the first stone was laid in mortar for the new two-story house of Francesco D'Amore, later to become mayor of Alberobello.[12] The fullest development of the once-crude *trullo* shelter had been achieved, for now construction with mortar was possible for all who could afford it.

The *trulli* were originally built by herders and farmers with the stones cleared from their fields. As the type became more refined, however, particularly during the period of rapid development when mortar was prohibited by law, *trullisti*, *trullo*-building specialists, took over the function of shelter construction on the Murgia, and *trullo* fabrication became a highly skilled craft.[13]

The raw material for a *trullo* could come from several possible sources. Loose stones from the field were one; quarried stone another. Often a large rainwater cistern or wine tank would be excavated in the rock beneath a *trullo*-to-be, and would yield a large quantity of good building stone. In later times especially, agricultural transformations were carried out, with great expenditure of labor, to make previously untillable land suitable for crops. The thin topsoil would be carefully removed and piled to one side, laying bare the limestone bedrock beneath. Then the limestone would be broken out in chunks to a depth of two or three feet. The best stones would be saved for construction, and the rest replaced over the still unbroken strata of the limestone, with the coarsest pieces on the bottom and the finest on the top. Following this back-breaking procedure, red *bolo* soil from a nearby depression would be carried to the field in baskets and tamped over the loose layers of broken limestone to a depth of fifteen or twenty inches. Finally, the original topsoil would be spread back over the *bolo*, and the land would be ready for cultivation. The heavy but sometimes infrequent rainfalls would be absorbed eagerly by the shallow topsoil and thick cushion of *bolo*, and once these soils had reached saturation the excess water would filter into the loose bed of broken rock beneath, from which, retained by the impervious bedrock, it could be slowly reabsorbed by the soil and roots above when needed. This continuous bed of limestone fragments, in addition to acting as an underground reservoir, served to furnish continual chemical fertilization to the soil from beneath, to complement the organic fertilizer added from above.[14]

On sloping land dry-laid retaining walls were often built of the stone to level the fields to an acceptable gradient. Stone boundary fences, also laid dry, with their two battered faces carefully assembled around a loose core of rock fragments, were universally built, often to a great thickness to use up excess stone. In many cases stone was still left over after all possible use had been made of it and was simply piled into great ricks in the fields.

The *trullista*, once supplied with stone, began his work by scraping bare the bedrock to serve as a foundation. If a cistern had been dug, it was capped with a lime-mortared barrel vault or dome which in many cases supported the floor of the house. The rectangular rooms were then carefully laid out, and the walls built much the same as the stone fences, with an inner plumb face, an outer, often battered face of carefully squared unmortared masonry, and a core of tamped rock fragments and soil. Tiny window openings were usually spanned with a lintel stone, but a doorway required a carefully made true arch of dry stonework. The thick walls were invariably hollowed in places by alcoves or niches which were spanned with unmortared barrel vaults, undoubtedly laid up with the aid of wood formwork.

As the construction of the vault began, a pole was erected and plumbed in the exact center of the room. A knotted cord attached to the pole gave an accurate radius to guide the placement of each stone. First the corners of the room were bridged by squinch courses until a full circular course had been achieved. Then the vault rose in horizontal rings, without formwork, each trimmed stone butted carefully against the stones on either side and projecting a predetermined amount over the ring of stones below. The tendency of the entire conical construction to collapse inward was resisted by the horizontal arch effect of each ring and by the horizontal friction forces between the rings. The pitch of the dome depended on the length of the stones used; longer stones could produce a flatter pitch.[15]

As this conical vault approached its apex, a large, heavy flat stone was used to close it and to anchor it down securely. Then the roofing, consisting of flat stones one to three inches in thickness called *chianche* or *chiancarelle*, sloped and overlapped to shed water, was added over the structural vault. Channels were provided to conduct rainwater from the roof down through the walls and into the cistern, from where it could be retrieved with a bucket and rope. *Chiancarelle* were also used, generally in a traditional rectilinear pattern, for the finished flooring of the house.

It has been theorized (and proved in the tholos tombs of Mycenae) that this seemingly precarious piling of loose masonry into a pseudo-dome could span rather large spaces. In practice, however, conditions seldom demanded very large spans, and the largest known space spanned *a trullo*, a wine room in Alberobello, measures but twenty feet square.[16]

The roofs of the *trulli*, whose limestone shingles have weathered to a dark grey, readily absorb and re-radiate solar heat, and are universally used for the drying of figs, tomatoes, *fave* beans, and other produce. To this end a *trullo* was often provided with one or more access stairways of stone constructed into its exterior walls. To provide for storage of dried foodstuffs, grain, flour, and miscellaneous household items the interior of the major dome in each house was fitted with a wooden *solaio* or *tavolato*, an attic platform at the level of the springing of the vault, reached by means of a wooden ladder. Except for the entrance door and lintel, this was the only wood used in the construction.

Sewage was distributed over the fields, working with the natural lime to increase the yield of the crops. In the town of Alberobello it was collected daily by a municipal removal service utilizing horses or mules with terra cotta jars slung over their backs; public sewers did not exist until 1932. Water from the Acquedotto Pugliese has been available in Alberobello since 1915, but even at present a number of houses still depend on their cisterns and the public fountains for water because of the high cost of trenching for pipes in the limestone hills on which the town rests. Rural *trullo*-dwellers still use cistern water exclusively.[17]

The immensely thick stone walls and dome of the *trullo*, pleasantly cool in the summer, tend to become unpleasantly cold during the winter months, condensing the moisture given off by cooking and breathing and making it difficult to feel warm even in front of the fire. To the present day cold walls are an accepted condition of life in all of southern Italy in the wintertime, in any type of house, *trullo* or otherwise, old or new. The inhabitants simply leave the doors open during the day to keep the interior dry, and live more outdoors than in, wearing numerous layers of clothing against the chill. Thermal insulation of buildings is unknown.

The same local limestone which turned dark when used on the roofs of the *trulli* became, if burned instead, the brilliant white medium for dealing with problems of light, cleanliness, and decoration. Lime plaster was used over the capstone of the conical vault to form first an apex for the cone, then a decorative pinnacle (*cucurneo* or *tintinule*) in some geometric or symbolic shape. In this particular undertaking, tradition allowed the builder considerable freedom of expression; to be sure the cap had a minor function as a flashing for the top of the dome, but the *cucurneo* itself served only to satisfy spiritual or personal needs of the builder-owner. Likewise the whitewashed symbols on the roofs had no physical function, but usually related to nonmaterial aspects of the occupant's life, be they of mystic or divine protection for the household, of individual aesthetic satisfaction or of ego satisfaction, of having a more cleverly decorated *trullo* than a neighbor.[18]

Through the long, Aegean-oriented history of Apulia and to the present day there have existed numerous cults of mystic and pagan religions, some having roots as old as Egypt, Assyria, and Babylonia. Thus, one may find pinnacles in the sphere-and-circle configuration, believed to be sun symbols inherited from primitive sun-worshippers who once inhabited the Salentine Peninsula; symbols of the zodiac whitewashed onto the stones of a roof; ciphers of the names of Christ and Mary, perhaps first painted on a *trullo* dome by medieval monks of the region and then copied for their clever forms by Christian and non-Christian alike; the swastika, still believed by many to be potent protection against the much-feared *malocchio* or "evil eye"; and other symbols of a protective nature, as well as more purely decorative ones.[19] Now one is likely to see graphic invocations of more immediate powers of protection such as an occasional cipher of an Italian political party, or the oft-seen "V.C." advertising to would-be thieves that the owner has paid for the nocturnal inspections of the *Vigilanza Campestra*, a public protection service.

Lime plaster was commonly, although not always, applied to the interior of a *trullo* for protection against drafts. In nearly all cases, except in *trulli* used for storage or stables, the interior was whitewashed, both for cleanliness and to make the most of the light entering through the open doorway and the tiny windows. Whitewashing of the exterior, except usually for the *chiancarelle* of the roof, is now universal in Alberobello and is very common in the surrounding countryside, although some of the most elegant rural *trulli* are made wholly of the natural stone without any finish whatsoever. Where whitewashing is done it is frequently the job of the housewives, usually preceding some local festival or another, and has become more a ritual than a necessity, perhaps to emphasize cleanliness, or perhaps to emphasize the separateness of the house from the landscape.

Despite the whiteness of the interior of the *trullo*, tasks such as mending, knitting, or stringing a basket of beans are best accomplished just outside the doorway, where the sun on the whitewashed walls casts a light of dazzling brightness. In many *trulli* the women simply put a chair just outside the door and sit, as modesty demands, facing into the house as they work. In many others outdoor spaces ranging upward from ten square feet in ground area, just large enough for a chair and its occupant, supplement the darker interior spaces. Some are furnished with a whitewashed outdoor stone table or bench built as an extension of the wall of the house. Even in seemingly crowded Alberobello, many *trulli* are also linked to generous walled gardens for growing grapes, fruit trees, or tomatoes, and raising chickens or rabbits.

The technique of the *trullo* was in many ways an ideal one. Because it utilized very small stones, it was quite adaptable to odd dimensions and shapes that might have been required in many situations. Its builders learned to roof almost any plan-shape with distorted *trullo* cones. *Trullo* chambers of varying sizes, amplified as necessary with nooks and niches, could be strung together in many ways to satisfy the simplest or most complex of needs. *Trulli* were cheaply built from available material. But there were also aspects that were less than ideal: the vast ground coverage of the walls; the inability to economically build structures of more than a single story; the unvarying need to roof every space with a tall cone requiring hundreds of hours of remarkably skilled, patient work. It was a moderately flexible technique but difficult, one which made its own expression the most prominent feature of any shelter which utilized it.

An enormous range of functions are housed in *trulli*. Single, crude domes serve as day-shelters for animal herders or field workers, or as sheds for sheep or goats. A haybarn is easily recognized by its truncated roof-cone, capped with a large, flat, removable stone, through which the barn is filled. Steps built into the roof afford the farmer easy access to this hatch. Slightly more refined single domes, or combinations of two or three domes, equipped with *cucine a terra* (open hearth kitchens) are often seasonal houses, used only during harvest time by growers of olives or grapes. Some in grape-growing areas house, in addition to basic living quarters, the press, subterranean storage tanks, and an aging room for the annual autumn production of wine. Year-round houses, in the country or in town, are often still larger and more complex. Entire farmsteads combine features of many of the above types in a single cluster: haybarns and animal barns, storehouses, dwelling units for the farmer and his clan.

Figure 1
A lone *trullo* sits amid
its terraced fields on the
northeastern flank of
the Murgia of the
Trulli, below Selva di
Fasano.

In the towns stores, workshops, bars, and offices are still found housed in *trulli*, although most commercial enterprises have already sought more modern quarters.

The *trullo* is a rural building type. With its immensely thick walls and its inability to form multistory structures, it is extremely wasteful of ground space, and in this way is ill-suited to high-density settlement, although being constructed of small stones it has a flexibility and adaptability of form which are extremely useful in tight urban situations. Outside the domain of the counts of Conversano *trullo* domes were built singly and in pairs, in groups of three or five, or sometimes in great farmyard clusters of a dozen or two dozen, but never for the occupancy of more than a single rural family who could spare the required land in exchange for a very inexpensive shelter. Towns were built of thin-walled, multistoried mortared stone structures. Within the domain of the counts, where mortar was outlawed, urban aggregations had to be made of *trulli*. More than two dozen *trullo* villages came into being with populations ranging upward from a dozen families. These can still be found on the rough, narrow dirt roads, away from the major towns of the Murgia: sleepy villages in various configurations, some with houses lined up along a single street, others clustered about a crossroads, others circling a generous common, usually to one side of the road which passes by. Nearly all are still inhabited; they bear names like Tumbinno, Paparello, San Marco Basso, Quei di Carlo, Cuccolicchio, and Caranna. A few are well preserved, but most have been rendered almost unrecognizable by newer buildings of *tufo* blocks and concrete slabs. One or two, like Neglia, are abandoned. Most have remained tiny, embryonic villages which are still alive but have never grown, nuclei of towns which will never be. Several, such as Cuccolicchio, have achieved populations which can be counted in hundreds. Only Alberobello, the brainchild of Gian Girolamo II, ever became a viable town.

The rural *trulli*, on cheaper land, ceased to be built when the cost of labor began to rise in the twentieth century. The sheer expense of handling the hundreds of tons of stone necessary for a single house became prohibitive. As new and lighter building techniques were developed for the towns of the Murgia, they were adopted also for rural use. Now, with the deaths of the last *trullisti*, *trullo* building is becoming a lost art.

Figure 2
A partially demolished *trullo* shows clearly the basic features of mature *trullo* construction. The cavity between the ashlar wall faces is filled with stone rubble. The inner wall face continues upward to become the structural vault and is covered with a layer of shingled *chiancarelle*.

Figure 3
A close view of an interior corner reveals the pendentive construction employed to make the transition from a square room to a conical dome. The apparently missing stone is actually a pocket intended for placement of a *solaio* pole. To the left is a mortarless barrel vault which spans a shallow alcove.

Figure 4
The typical double door
lintel construction
consists of a stone
arch and a flat lintel of
wood and stone. The
arch carries the
structural dome and
most of the load,
whereas the flat lintel,
enabling insertion of a
square door, bears only
a few infill stones and
chiancarelle.

Figure 5
The fine workmanship
and complex
stereotomy of a
developed *trullo* dome
are apparent in this
straight-upward view.

Figure 6
A farmhouse near Selva di Fasano faces on a sunny dooryard where most of the household chores are done. Drawings of this house are shown in Fig. 22.

Figure 7
A house near Laureto.

Figure 8
A house near Pezzolla,
one of the small *trullo*
villages.

Figure 9
A rudimentary field
shelter between Ceglie
Messapico and San
Vito dei Normanni has
its roof whitewashed as
well as its walls.

Following pages
Figures 10 and 11
In some cases *trullo*
domes are plastered
over, particularly if
there is a leakage
problem. This house is
in the countryside south
of Cisternino, immedi-
ately across the road
from the Specchia
Sativa and a remaining
piece of the Paretone.

Figure 12
In the vicinity of Ostuni
can be found many
shelters which are
vaulted with true domes
and completely
plastered and white-
washed. See Fig. 24.

Figure 13
A farmhouse south of
Cisternino.

Figure 14
A farm complex south
of Martina Franca.

Figure 15
A farm complex near
Cisternino.

Figure 16
A farm complex near
Selva di Fasano.
Toward the left, a
trullo for hay storage
can be identified by its
truncated top and its
outside access stairway.

Figure 17
Trulli are often seen in
combination with later
types of construction.
This group, in the small
village of Lamie
Affascinate, includes a
two-story barrel-
vaulted structure of
mortared masonry. The
vault is covered with a
double-pitched roof of
chiancarelle.

Figure 18
This abandoned *trullo*, in the countryside south of Martina Franca, was built in two stages. The large circular chamber to the left is older and less refined in its construction. The axis of its doorway is skewed away from the center of the room, perhaps to give a larger protected space to one side of its interior. A small smoke hole is provided at the summit of its vault. The newer addition to the right shows greater sophistication in its square interior plan and vaulted alcoves, although it still retains the rudimentary smoke hole. An outside stairway at the rear ascends to the roof.

Figure 19
A transitional form of *trullo* field shelter, nonrectilinear in plan. A main space is joined to a smaller one housing a fireplace. Such shelters are often found with two or three smaller spaces attached to the main space, as illustrated in the small sketches. (Plan and section courtesy *Byggekunst*, redrawn by the author.)

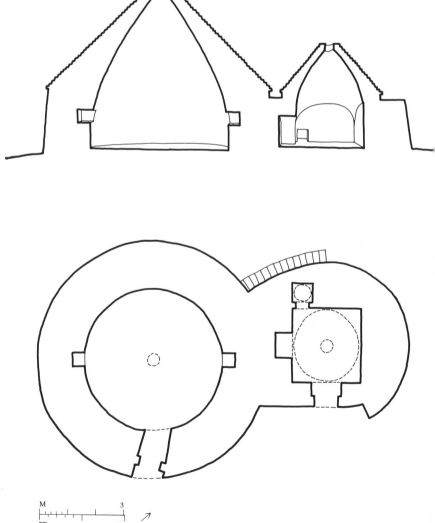

M   3
FT   10

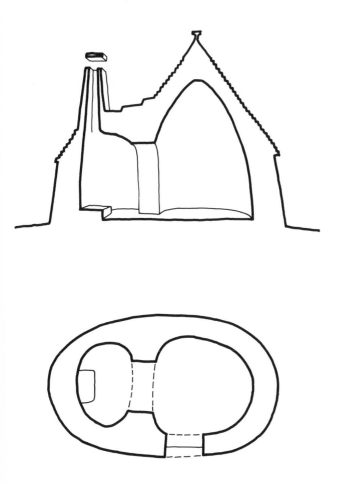

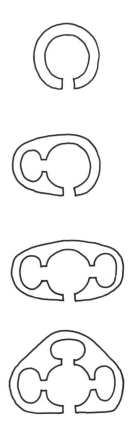

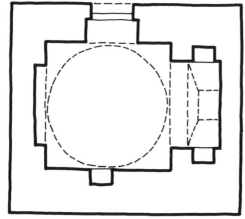

M
3

FT
10

Figure 20
This field shelter of
mature *trullo* construc-
tion stands in an olive
grove near Alberobello.
Its layout and work-
manship are very
precise. The dome
construction of this
shelter is illustrated in
Fig. 5.

Figure 21
This farmhouse by the
town forest of
Alberobello has one
atypical feature, the
indoor oven which
shows in the upper
right-hand corner of the
plan. An oven is more
commonly built outside
the house, to avoid
heating the living
quarters during hot
weather. The largest
dome covers the main
living space. The
kitchen is a large open
hearth whose covering
dome leads to a
chimney. Two bed-
rooms, each with a tiny
window and a storage
niche, complete the
house. A barrel-vaulted
woodbox opens to the
outside from the space
beneath the oven.
Solaio poles without
platforms occur in all
three major rooms.

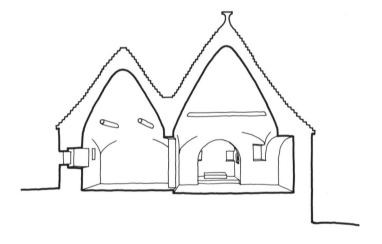

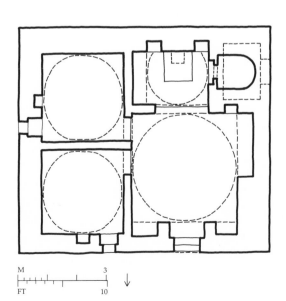

Figure 22
The three rooms across
the back of this farm-
house, one of them
barrel-vaulted, are all
used for storage at the
present time. The
bedroom at center right
has no outside window
only an opening into
the adjacent kitchen.
The outside room by
the kitchen window
houses rabbits.
Chickens are raised in a
low, crude *trullo* of
their own just off this
drawing to the left. The
cistern is under the
front courtyard. For a
photograph of this
house, see Fig. 6.

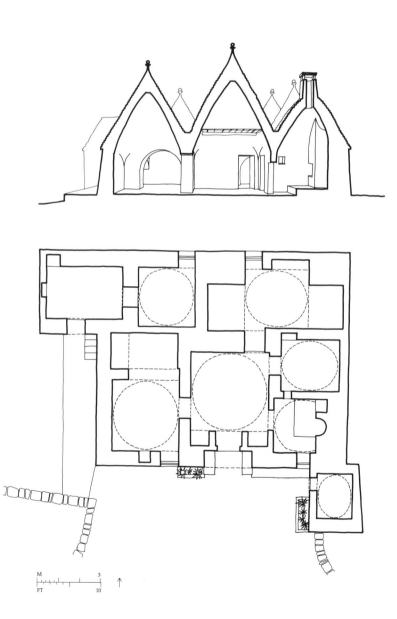

Figure 23
In the Valley of Itria and the area south of Martina Franca are found *trulli* constructed specifically for the making of wine. In this example, the entrance doorway leads to a living space served by a bed alcove and a *cucina a terra*. The house is occupied only during the grape harvest, so these accommodations are not lavish. The lower half of the *trullo,* covered by two domes, is the pressroom.

Grapes are dumped in through the large window to the right, and are squeezed in the press at the left. The juice runs onto the sloping stone floor and into a sump, from which it is allowed to drain into one of two large, plastered tanks which are hewn from the underlying rock. The larger tank holds fifty-four *suma,* more than seven thousand liters. Hatches in the floor permit withdrawal of wine from the tanks. Rainwater is collected

from the roof and conducted by a metal pipe down the front wall to a barrel-vaulted cistern under the door-yard patio. From there it may be withdrawn through a square hatch and dumped into the adjoining stone tank, from which it is dipped out in buckets and carried to the grape-vines during dry weather. Two stairways allow access to the roof for the drying of figs and tomatoes. A frequently seen feature is the summer kitchen,

a crude *trullo* dome appended to the house to allow cooking to take place without heating the interior of the house.

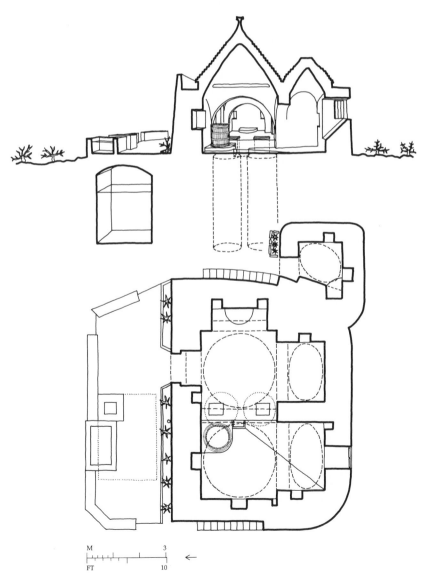

M ⊢┼┼┼┼┼ 3
FT ⊢┼┼┼┼┼┼┼ 10 ←

Figure 24
An example of the
true-dome type of
shelter found in the
vicinity of Ostuni.

Figure 25
The locations of *trullo*
villages on the Murgia
of Trulli.

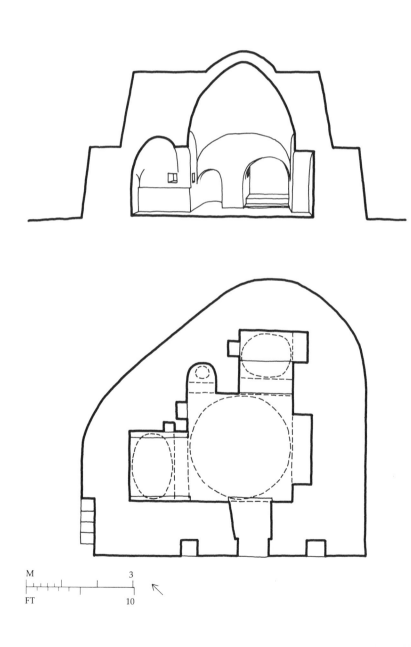

M   3

FT   10

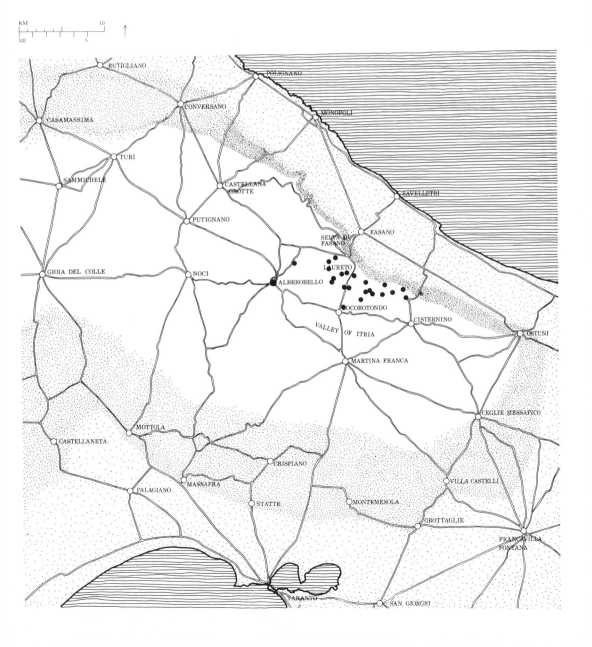

Figure 26
Cuccolicchio, seen here
from the ridgetop near
Selva di Fasano, is
typical of the small,
multifamily aggrega-
tions of *trulli* which
may be found on the
Murgia. Directly above
it, near the horizon, is
Ianelle, another tiny
trullo village. Most such
towns have been
considerably altered by
recent construction.

Figure 27
The road into Pezzolla,
another *trullo* village.

ure 28
Rione Monti of
erobello. (Photo-
ph courtesy Conces.
339 del 29/8/64
o Stato Maggiore
onautica Militare.)

ure 29

lan of the Rione
nti of Alberobello,
larger of the two
rters of the city that
preserved as
ional monuments.
black shapes are
buildings, almost
of them *trulli*. The
ain rises steeply
m the long market
are at the north
ard the south.
ording to Sisto and
giulli this quarter
upies about 37 acres,
ludes 1,030 *trulli*,
l houses 3,000
abitants.

M   50

FT   150

Figures 30 and 31
Two Alberobello streets
climb the hill in long,
sloping steps of
limestone paving
blocks.

Figures 32 and 33
Alberobello.

Figures 34 and 35
Alberobello.

Following pages
Figure 36
Alberobello.

Figure 37
This Alberobello
dooryard serves to
collect rainwater and
funnel it into the
cistern whose vault
rises above the
surrounding paving.

Figure 38
An Alberobello
dooryard.

Figure 39
Tiny birdcages are hung
in Alberobello door-
ways in the morning
and taken in at night.

Following pages
Figures 40 and 41
Alberobello.

Figure 42
Rainwater gutters on an
Alberobello house lead
to a collection box. The
drain hole to the
outside is plugged until
the subfloor cistern has
been filled through an
interior pipe.

Figure 43
A group of very modest
Alberobello houses in
the Rione Aia Piccola.

M   3
FT   10

Figure 44
This house in the Rione Aia Piccola of Alberobello was squeezed into a tight corner location. The main room is flanked by a skewed bedroom on one side and a dining room with two bed alcoves on the other. A *cucina a terra* completes the house. It has no garden.

Figure 45
The Alberobello house, in the Rione Monti, has a small walled garden just outside its kitchen door. The largest room is used for eating and sleeping. Next to it, opening to the street, is a small living room connected to a cloister-vaulted bedroom. An angled stairway has been constructed to convert the former cistern into a cellar. The existence of a small second kitchen adjacent to the living room suggests that this house is a combination of two smaller ones, the "front" one with small kitchen, living room, and bedroom, and the "back" one with the garden, an entrance where the stairway is now, the large room, and the kitchen.

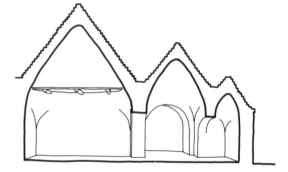

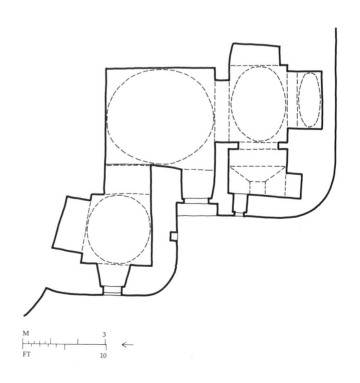

M   3
FT   10   ←

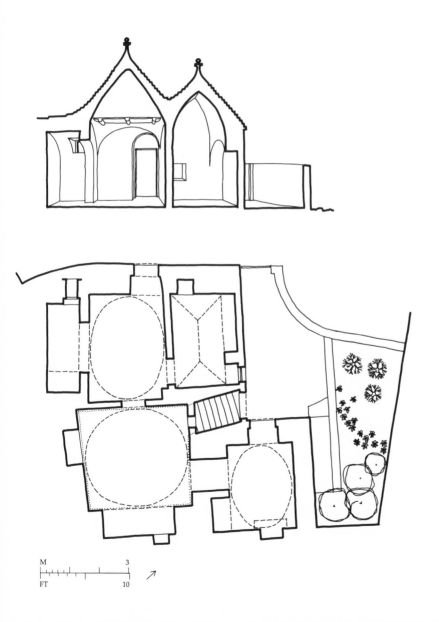

Figure 46
Another house in the
Rione Monti has three
bedrooms and a kitchen
opening from the main
room. An outdoor
garden, now occupied
by a gift shop, was once
reached from the
kitchen. A spiral stair
between the kitchen
and the main entrance
descends to a converted
cistern whose bucket
hatchway is still
visible in the kitchen.

Figure 47
Three well-constructed
trullo domes catch the
light of the late
afternoon sun.

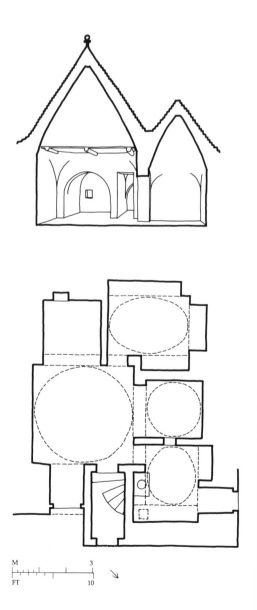

M   3
FT   10

V

Of Mortared Stone: Cisternino

In the eighth century A.D. a band of Basilian monks, fleeing like their brothers at Massafra from persecution in the East, landed on the Adriatic shore of Apulia. They crossed the plain, made their way up the slope to the Murgia of the Trulli, and began looking for a site on which to build a monastery.

They settled eventually upon an airy hilltop between the Valley of Ibernia and the broad Valley of Itria. They named their monastery San Nicolo di Patara cis-Sturninum.[1] The "cis-Sturninum" told the location of the monastery: just beyond the ruins of the ancient town of Sturninum, which were then a well-known landmark. In common usage the place was soon known as Cisturninum, which in time evolved into the name Cisternino, by which it is presently known.

Like most monasteries of the time, the one at Cisternino quickly became a center of teaching and healing for the farm families of the surrounding valleys. A village soon grew about the monastery, and when the monstery was later destroyed by marauders, the continually expanding community grew over its ruins as it began to crowd the hilltop.

The earliest known document concerning the town of Cisternino, from the year 1180, establishes that it was governed at that time by the bishop of Monopoli. Except for a brief later period when its control was sold by one of the bishops to a secular baron, and despite a popular revolt in 1667 which culminated in the destruction of the bishop's palace opposite the church, Cisternino continued to be a feudal possession of the bishops of Monopoli under various conquerors until 1807, when Joseph Bonaparte, king of Naples, ended the practice of feudalism in southern Italy. Bishops of Monopoli even now bear the title of baron of Cisternino, and the coat of arms of the town still exhibits a bishop's crosier between two roses which symbolized the religious and civil jurisdictions of the bishop.

Between 1505 and 1528 Cisternino was under Venetian rule. The marquis of Vasto, commanding Spanish troops, then succeeded in driving out the Venetians, and began a century and a half of Spanish rule which ended in the long-lasting wars of succession and the subsequent Italian unification movement.

In the thirteenth century the Anjou kings of Naples built defensive walls around the hilltop of Cisternino, as they did around many other towns of the Murgia of the Trulli. In the mid-fifteenth century, under the Spaniards, the walls were rebuilt and strengthened, with towers at the four corners and at the main gate by the church. By the early seventeenth century, however, such walls were of little further military value, and the town began to expand down the gentle southeasterly slope outside its walls. Eventually most of the defensive works were torn down, until today only two towers and a few remnants of wall remain, all converted to residential occupancy.

In our century Cisternino has not only continued its southeastward expansion, but has also pushed out toward the northwest and even down the precipitous northeastern slope. Two large town parks on the steep southwestern flank, facing the Valley of Itria, have curtailed development in that direction. The old town is now almost hidden from the outside by new construction, but from its interior it is evident that it is still contained as if by its walls, and has changed but little during the past several centuries.

Cisternino, once famous for its annual farmer's fair, still remains an agricultural center, a collection of tiny stores, workshops, and residences with no large industry. Within the outline of the walls the only large public structures are the church, remodeled in the nineteenth century, and the bishop's palace opposite, still a gutted ruin from the revolt of 1667. The rest of the town consists of small cells of living and working space squeezed together and stacked high along narrow streets to make best use of the scarce space within the fortifications.

In its early days, before the erection of the walls, Cisternino may well have been a primitive village of simple wood *capanne*, like many others. With the building of the fortifications, however, a new and more suitable building technique had to be found for the shelters within, one which allowed building walls to be thin, yet to support several upper stories. Permanence, incombustibility, and flexibility of planning within the tight townspace were also desirable. Cheapness was essential.

Monolithic, mortared, true vaulting of masonry was the answer. It was thin, strong, could be made to span almost any shape or size of space, and would last for centuries. Limestone could be easily quarried anywhere, even from the hill on which the town stood. Small blocks could be cut for construction, and the irregular, broken pieces burned in kilns to produce lime which, when mixed with *bolo* soil, made a cheap and serviceable mortar. The materials were at hand, and labor cost but little.

Wood was also available for construction. It was used to make formwork for the vaults,[2] and as fuel for the lime kilns. But it was never used structurally in the mature shelters of Cisternino, nor in those of the other similar towns of the Murgia. Floors, ceilings, roofs, balconies, stairs—all could be made economically of stone, and the results were functionally much more satisfactory than with wood.

The exact origin of the art of making true vaults as it was practiced in Cisternino and her sister cities of the Murgia of the Trulli is uncertain. Most certainly the Romans built vaulted warehouses and dwellings in Bari and Brindisi. Most certainly the French and Spaniards were masters of the full and complex range of Gothic vault forms during the periods in which they controlled Cisternino. Probably all three contributed to the knowledge with which Cisternino was built.

The masons of Cisternino were men of exceptional ingenuity. They sometimes laid up walls of regular stone blocks, but in other cases made walls by compacting irregular stones and mortar between wood forms.³ Their combinations of arches and vaults were often graceful and correct, but more often were brutally expedient, and were most often full-blooded, lusty, folk-art inventions that made some charmingly naïve concessions to grace and correctness. Nothing was sacred to the masons but the sheer physical stability of what they built. A half-arch could support a stair, a tilted barrel vault could cover it. A round barrel vault could be intersected by pointed-vault dormers. A triangular piece of vaulting could support a diagonal balcony front if held at its vertex on a projecting stone bracket. A buttress to a building across the street could resist the excessive thrust of a roof vault, or of a too-ambitiously cantilevered balcony. An irregular room shape was easily covered with a skewed vault. Almost anything could be supported or spanned by cutting, twisting, tilting, truncating, or combining the standard forms of vaulting in nonstandard ways.

This ragbag patchwork technique was ideal for its purpose. Mortared stone construction was strong, impervious to rain and wind, and when whitewashed was quite satisfactory in appearance from either interior or exterior. Its poor performance as a thermal insulator was not a serious drawback, for no system had yet been invented which was better in that regard. As with the *trulli*, the house or shop was left open to the breeze, summer or winter, to avoid condensation on the walls, and everyday activities were carried out at the ambient temperature whether indoors or out.

The flexibility of this system of construction was unsurpassed in its time. Because each building was composed of thousands of small pieces, it could be made in any shape or dimension to satisfy whim, need, or the restrictions of available space. The finished structure was of a single piece, but could be added to or altered at any time and the scars of the surgery instantly healed with an application of whitewash. Vertical and horizontal multiplication of spaces was possible, or a space could be readily subdivided if required. The easy availability of the necessary materials and the low cost of labor made the system cheap, and thereby assured its automatic, unquestioned, universal adoption.

Only in two respects did the system require particular care on the part of the builder. Its vaults could be warped, segmented, or combined in strange ways, but they had to be curved against their superimposed loads, and they had to be buttressed adequately against the resulting lateral thrusts. These were minor inconveniences to the skilled mason and his client, but they alone were sufficient to guarantee a certain constancy of form among the disparate structures of the town, built to widely varying requirements in an almost perfectly plastic technique.

The resulting shelters range from the very simple and unpretentious to some fairly elaborate and ostentatious dwellings. Almost all are basically single-floor apartments which are stacked above or below others in narrow two- or three-story buildings. Most are quite constricted in floor area, so those on the upper floors avoided further diminution by having their access stairs outside the building, in the already-narrow street. These exterior stairs are the pride of the town—"*uno spettacolo di scale*"—and are often as ornamental as they are functional. In a number of cases entire buildings are arched over the streets a story or two above the pavement. Further use of outdoor space is often achieved on the upper floor levels by brightly flower-festooned balconies, or by carved stone brackets on either side of a window which can hold potted plants. Another common feature is a pair of pierced stone brackets just above a window, once used to hold a pole for clothes-drying. The window frame itself is ornamentally carved in some cases, but several centuries of annual whitewashing have softened the once-sharp relief sculptures and have rendered many of them almost unrecognizable.

Inside, the simpler houses consist of one or two rooms, often with lofts or attics. They are equipped much the same as a *trullo*, with a simple *cucina a terra* for cooking, and a bucket hole, often even on the upper floors, through which water can be drawn from a subterranean cistern. Wall niches of all shapes and sizes are common. Sewage was originally removed daily from the household in jars, but now the Acquedotto Pugliese, sewers, and electricity serve the town, and a growing number of families are finding corners in which to install a flush toilet and a washbasin. Floors were originally of *chiancarelle* as in the *trulli*, though many houses have been refloored with terrazzo tile. The interior walls and vaults are coated with whitewash, *latte di calcio*, and, as on the exterior, the accumulated layers of several centuries have often reached a considerable thickness.

Each building is roofed with limestone, many with steeply sloping gabled *chiancarelle* roofs, others with flatter pitches of carefully trimmed and fitted slabs, tightly mortared together. The runoff water is channeled into the basement cistern. The whitewash of the exterior walls must, by law, be renewed in May or June of each year. Often this is done by the housewife, and in other instances by a roving professional *imbianchino* with a very long-handled brush.

The walled town could originally be entered only through the Porta Piccola (Small Gate) to the northeast or the Porta Grande (Large Gate) between the bishop's palace and the church on the southwest. The two gates, still the main entrances, are connected by a narrow main street which runs through a piazza, originally about a third of its present size, in the center of town. A meandering circular route connects the quarters of the town to each other and to the main street. From these two major routes numerous closed alleys serve various clusters of houses. The streets, none sufficiently wide for vehicular traffic, are paved with slabs of limestone polished smooth by millions of footsteps. They traverse deep clefts between the tall, narrow buildings, coolly shaded on the hottest summer day but bright and cheerful in the brilliant light reflected from the white facades. For twenty-three hours of the day the streets are faultlessly clean, often scrubbed with water and brush. But after lunch household rubbish is pitched from the windows, and while the townspeople sleep off their wine and food in the heat of the early afternoon, a busy crew of street cleaners tidy the pavements and everyone awakes to a clean town.

Since the demolition of the walls several new entrances have been cut into the southeastern half of the town, connecting it with the new piazza to the southeast and tunneling through the town wall toward the southwest. The entire northwestern half of the town has but one new avenue of access, behind the bishop's palace.

For several hundred years, until well into the twentieth century, stone vaulting was the major building technique of the Murgia of the Trulli. In its first century or two it was used for the construction of the magnificent white hill towns: Ostuni, the White Queen of the Olives; Martina Franca, dazzling in its baroque detail, envied for its palace by Bernini, to this day circled by its old wall and towers; Locorotondo, of the strong and simple house forms; Cisternino, the City of Stairs; Noci, Putignano, Castellana Grotte, Ceglie Messapico, Carovigno. Only Alberobello and its smaller cousins, by political order, were built by another technique.

During the last century, the construction of vaulting on the Murgia of the Trulli began to change. *Tufo* blocks were increasingly substituted for limestone. Buildings, even simple ones, became more classical in style, and their vaulting became correspondingly more self-conscious and regular in shape. A few new buildings are still being vaulted with *tufo* at the time of this writing. But the majority are spanned in another material, fully as durable, even more flexible, and quicker and cheaper to erect. That material is reinforced concrete.

Figure 1
A simple two-story field shelter of vaulted stone sits abandoned in a vineyard between Locorotondo and Cisternino. Flat floors and roof pitches are produced by infilling over the curved vaults.

Figure 2
A ruined field shelter in the Valley of Itria demonstrates the basic features of true vaulted construction. The vault is thin, and its stones are placed radially from the geometric center of the vault. The wall is thick, to buttress the thrust of the vault, and consists of two carefully laid faces with a core of broken stone. The whole construction is bound together with a weak mortar of *bolo* soil and lime.

Figure 3
This series of vaulted
buildings is found on
the edge of Alberobello.

Figure 4
A farmstead near
Alberobello includes
three types of con-
struction: *trullo* vaults
to the left, mortared
barrel vaults covered
by gable roofs to the
right, and a flat-roofed
construction of
reinforced concrete in
the center.

Figures 5 and 6
The farmstead of
Monte Tre Carlini near
Locorotondo

Figure 7
The farmstead of
Monte Tre Carlini near
Locorotondo dates from
1750, and is one of the
largest and most
impressive of the
region. Its balcony is
a particularly fine
construction of
corbelled stone.

Figure 8
This barrel-vaulted
house stands in
Alberobello. To the
left on entering are a
cucina a terra and a bed
alcove; in the front
corner to the right is a
hatch opening to a
subfloor cistern. The
rear room is a bedroom,
and the ample loft
above is also used for
sleeping. The vault over
the loft is pointed. Both
portions of the house
are covered by gabled
roofs of *chiancarelle*.

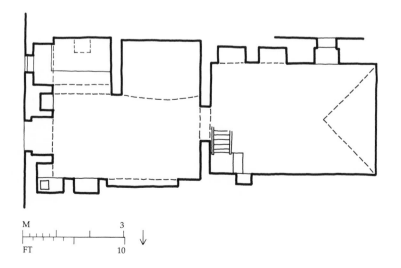

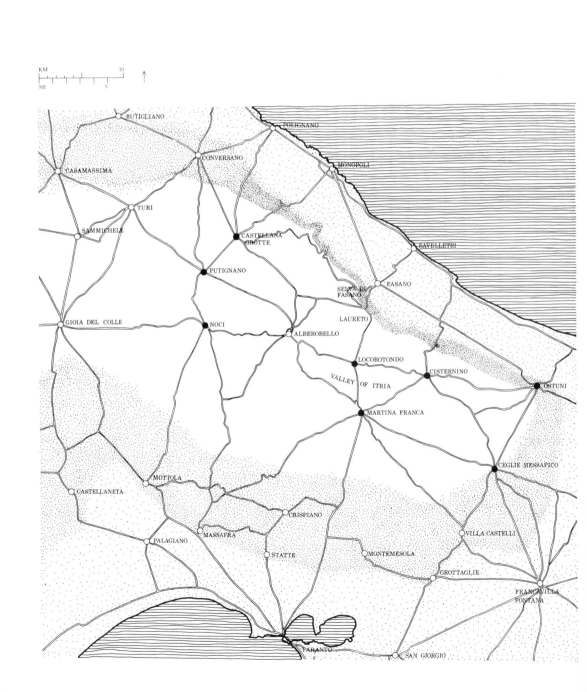

KM   10

MI   5

RUTIGLIANO

POLIGNANO

CONVERSANO

MONOPOLI

CASAMASSIMA

TURI

SAMMICHELE

CASTELLANA
GROTTE

SAVELLETRI

PUTIGNANO

FASANO

SELVA DI
FASANO

GIOIA DEL COLLE

LAURETO

NOCI

ALBEROBELLO

LOCOROTONDO

CISTERNINO

OSTUNI

VALLEY OF ITRIA

MARTINA FRANCA

CEGLIE MESSAPICO

MOTTOLA

CASTELLANETA

CRISPIANO

VILLA CASTELLI

MASSAFRA

PALAGIANO

STATTE

MONTEMESOLA

GROTTAGLIE

FRANCAVILLA
FONTANA

TARANTO

SAN GIORGIO

Figure 9
Nearly all existing
towns of the Murgia of
the Trulli were built of
stone with the use of
mortar.

Figure 10
The old town of
Cisternino. The black
shapes are the
buildings, and the
dotted lines indicate
where the buildings are
arched over the streets.
The exact location of
all of the encircling
wall is not known, but
it followed roughly
along the backs of the
houses to the north-
west, across the south-
western edge of the
town, along the inside
face of the long piazza
on the southeastern
side, and inside the
detached block of
houses and the street to
the northeast. The
Porta Grande is next
to the church on the
southwest, and the
Porta Piccola lies at the
northeastern end of the
main street.

Figure 11
This small office, once
a blacksmith shop, lies
close to the Porta
Piccola on the ground
floor of a building.

Figure 12
The simplest Cisternino
house is a single barrel-
vaulted chamber. This
example is slightly
more elaborate, with a
loft supported by two
segmental barrel vaults
running perpendicular
to the axis of the main
vault. These two
vaults are intersected
by an arch which spans
the alcoves in the back
wall. Except for a tiny
window in the end wall
over the loft, the
doorway furnishes all
light and air for the
dwelling. Food is
cooked in a simple
cucina a terra next to
the doorway.

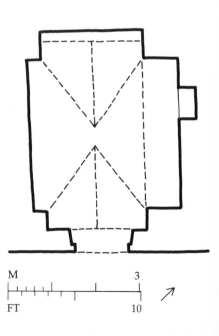

M 3
FT 10

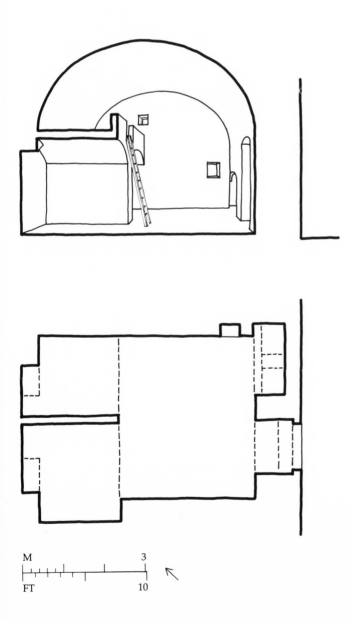

M   3
|—+——+——+——+——+——+——+——|
FT   10

Figure 13
Basically similar in its
plan, this house uses a
more elaborate main
vault form, probably
primarily as a means of
decreasing the amount
of infill required to
produce a level floor
above.

Figure 14
Carved stone
ornamentation and
more complex forms of
vaulting are
characteristic of many
houses in Cisternino.
Here are seen orna-
mental pilasters below
a rather flat domed
vault in the living room,
and a similar vault over
the low attic. The
trapezoidal bedroom is
covered by a cloister
vault, and barrel vaults
span the tiny kitchen
and the generous
balcony. This house is
on the second floor of a
three-story building,
and has an exterior
access stairway.

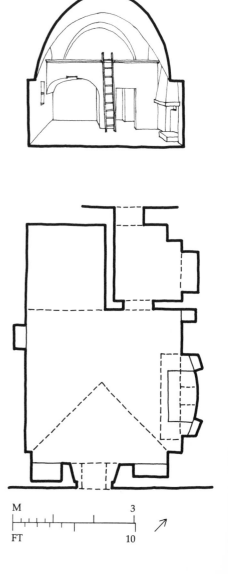

M   3
├┼┼┼┼┼───────┤   ↗
FT   10

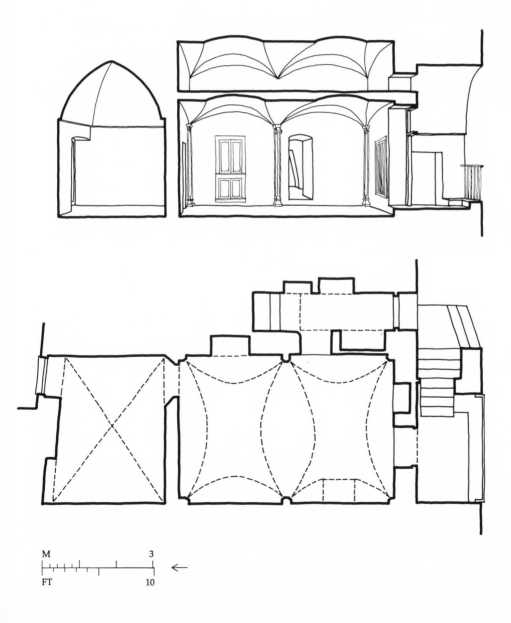

M   3
|—|—|—|—|—|——|——| ←
FT   10

Figure 15
This second-floor
house, also with an
exterior stairway,
shows many overt
attempts at achieving
elegance. Its vaulting is
pretentiously complex
and is ornamented in
one of the bedrooms
with shallow ribs. The
horizontal moldings in
the living room do not
meet at the corners. The
kitchen, however, is
still a simple *cucina
a terra*.

Figure 16
Cisternino.

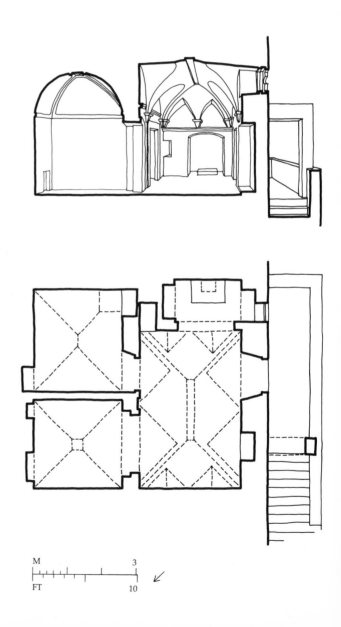

M   3

FT   10

Figures 33 and 34
Cisternino.

Figures 35 and 36
Cisternino.

Figures 41 and 42
Cisternino.

Figures 43 and 44
Cisternino.

Figures 47 and 48
Cisternino.

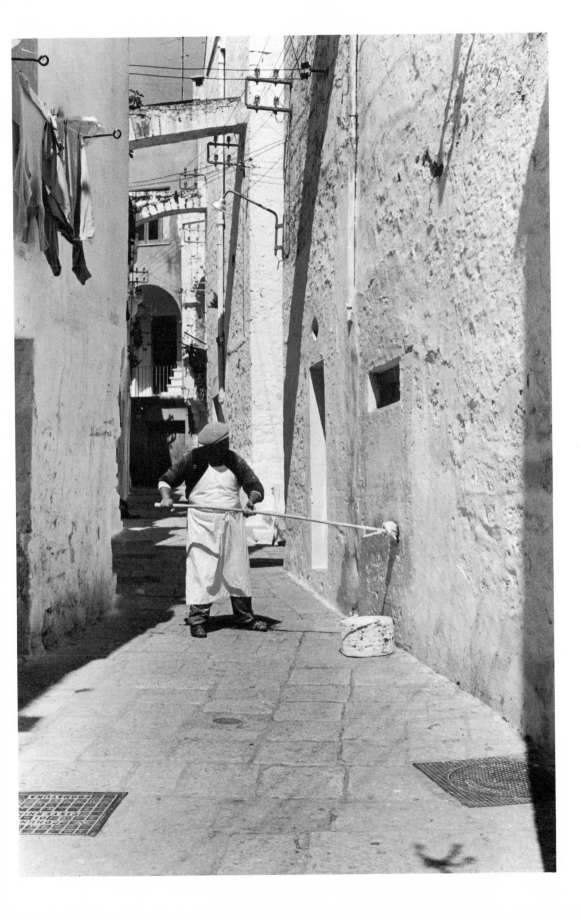

VI

Superstone

The twentieth century has brought rapid change to the Murgia of the Trulli. During the first three decades a large number of its inhabitants emigrated to the United States.[1] First under fascism, then under the Christian Democratic party after the Second World War, water, electricity, sewers, and paved roads were brought to its towns and countryside, and parks and public buildings were constructed. In the postwar period veterans were put to work converting more of its rocky fields to fertile cropland. Agricultural productivity rose to new levels, and incomes began to rise faster than prices.

Until the Second World War most construction had been done by the traditional methods. New *trulli* still rose among the vines and olive trees of the fields. Mortared vaulting of *tufo* blocks roofed the new buildings of the towns. But with the postwar boom came change. The old houses were adequate enough, for domestic life did not change appreciably, but where a new house was required it could not be built by the old techniques. A man's time had become worth something, and a five-hundred-ton *trullo* could no longer be built as cheaply as a newer type of house that required only a fourth as much material to be lifted and put into place. Of even greater impact were the new types of shelters which suddenly had to be built on the Murgia: sheds for mechanized agricultural equipment, small factories for wine and oil cooperatives, hotels, schools and hospitals, larger retail stores, and repair garages for automobiles. These were larger, longer-span structures, quite different in their spatial requirements from the old buildings. They required new techniques, lighter and stronger, quicker and more flexible, able to be added to older buildings or to rise independently on new ground.

Wood as a primary building material had not been used on the Murgia of the Trulli since before the construction of the walled towns. It had become scarce and expensive as agriculture took over the last of the forest lands in Apulia. Steel was more expensive than wood, and required expensive precision tools for its fabrication. But the price of concrete was within reason. As a material it was not as cheap as *tufo* blocks or hollow clay tiles on a volumetric basis, but its erection was fast and simple, and with selective placement of a few strands of steel it could do anything, span anything, and support anything.

The typical postwar, present-day building of the Murgia rests on shallow concrete foundations bedded in the underlying stone. Its floor is a thin concrete slab, perhaps faced with ceramic or terrazzo tile, poured over carefully compacted layers of lime-stabilized earth. Its walls are of *tufo* blocks, hollow concrete blocks, or in some cases hollow clay tiles trucked in from towns outside the Murgia. In most instances its walls are loadbearing, although frequently concrete columns are poured to carry the load and the walls become only screens. The roof at its simplest is a flat slab of poured-in-place concrete reinforced with steel rods, formed on a crude platform of boards supported by rough wood poles. For greater economy, a ribbed slab can be produced by pouring the concrete over spaced parallel rows of hollow clay tiles laid on stringers. In recent years crudely made precast tee-slabs, small in cross-section and prestressed with wires, have also come into common use for floor and roof structures. Carefully proportioned transit-mixed concrete is unknown. If not mixed with shovels, the concrete is made in miniscule batches of dubious consistency in a small power mixer, and is often carried to the roof on the backs of apprentices who lug it in buckets up the long wooden ladders. Larger mixers and tall construction cranes, however, are coming gradually into use.

When the last block is laid on the parapet, if there is still money left in the budget, the walls are smoothly stuccoed inside and out, hiding effectively the various materials beneath and rendering the walls impervious. Sometimes they are then whitewashed, but inexpensive paints are now available. Pastel colors are preferred. The roof is surfaced with asphalt built-up roofing. Doors and window frames are of wood.

This is functionally an admirable type of construction. Although the slab work and the masonry are generally done very rapidly and crudely, they are nevertheless more than sufficiently strong, and the concealing qualities of the stucco allow even plumbing, roof drains, and wiring to be efficiently installed in rough gouged-out chases. In the end it is a sturdy, monolithic whole. It need not be modular or even rectangular; both the concrete and the easily cut wall blocks can be erected in any shape or dimension. For this reason the technique has found great popularity in the usage of odd-shaped vacant lots in the towns, and in the addition of new rooms to old *trulli*. It can be utilized for very large single-story warehouses, or for very tall apartment buildings. Buildings of six or more floors are now quite common on the outskirts of the Murgia towns.

In short, with concrete nothing is impossible. It is superstone. It is perfectly plastic. Flat, cantilevered, arched, or reverse-curved, it has no weakness that cannot be cured with hidden strands of steel. In theory it can be built as high or as wide as one wishes, in any shape, within limits so broad as to be meaningless. It is also the most economical material of construction now in use on the Murgia.

In practice, the concrete buildings of the Murgia of the Trulli are seldom more formally complex than flat-topped rectangular boxes, whether single boxes alone in fields or several dozen boxes stacked together as apartments. Attempts at ornamentation are universal and vary wildly in form. Some of the more common ones are fancy balcony railings of concrete or wrought iron, colored ceramic tile facings, and cut-stone moldings around windows and doors.

As yet there is no urban complex of these new boxes which can be logically compared with Massafra, Alberobello, or Cisternino. In quantity, concrete structures may already outnumber the combined total of caves, *trulli*, and vaulted stone shelters of the Murgia, but there is no current need for entire new towns. The new concrete buildings instead are built around the old towns, circling them in numerous rings of slab dwelling towers and low, broad shops and factories, and infiltrating the towns as their older buildings are torn down. Concrete is infiltrating the old towns at a smaller scale as well, in such guises as a new flat-slab *solaio* platform in a *trullo*, in place of a rotted one of wood poles, or a neatly tapered, iron-railed cantilevered balcony in Cisternino, replacing a crumbling construction of corbelled and arched limestone. It is cheaper, stronger, and more long-lasting than wood in a *solaio*, or stone in a balcony.

In time, barring major technological change, in the course of natural urban growth and regeneration processes, concrete will produce its own towns on the Murgia of the Trulli. Probably most of these towns will have no more professional design skill exercised in their construction than did Massafra, Alberobello, or Cisternino. Like these three older towns, each of them will represent in its form and details the aggregate of thousands of small, independent design decisions made by individual inhabitants and their builders. Yet it is already evident that a concrete town will never possess the qualities which relate Massafra, Alberobello, and Cisternino to one another, and which make the three of them unmistakably towns of the Murgia.

Why not? Each of the four techniques—*tufo* caves, *trulli*, mortared stone vaulting, and reinforced concrete—represents a way of building which was or is cheapest and most flexible under a certain set of conditions. Each is basically a single-material, monochromatic technique. But in the caves all construction had to relate to the face of the cliff. In the *trulli* every space had to be roofed with a conical dome. Vaults of mortar and stone had to be curved and buttressed against the loads they were to carry. In each of these three cases a fundamental limitation of the technique produced a basic architectonic form of which all shelters had to be variations. The fourth case, concrete, is a technique without limitations, and it imparts no basic form. It will not produce a Massafra, an Alberobello, or a Cisternino. It will instead produce towns without souls.

Figure 1
In 1928 the Rione
Monti of Alberobello,
pictured in Fig. 28 of
Chapter IV, was
declared a national
monument, and its
development arrested.
This is a photograph of
an unprotected portion
of Alberobello which
was taken in 1964. The
Rione Monti may be
seen in the background.
Further new construc-
tion has occurred since
the taking of this
picture. (Photograph
courtesy Conces. No.
339 del 29/8/64 dello
Stato Maggiore
Aeronautica Militare.)

Appendix 1: The Drawings and Photographs

Except as noted, all photographs and drawings were made by the author. The Touring Club Italiano guidebook *Puglia* and detailed topographic maps from the Istituto Geografico Militare were of great assistance in plotting the thousands of miles of travel on the back roads of Apulia which were essential to this effort. The guidebook is available from any T.C.I. office in Italy, and the maps may be purchased from the Galleria dei Libri on Via Nazionale in Rome.

In each provincial capital of Italy the Ufficio Catasto (tax assessor's office) sells detailed maps of the towns in its province. These maps show the outline of each building, and were used in the construction of the maps of Alberobello and Cisternino in this volume. The Gravina of the Madonna della Scala at Massafra has never been mapped in detail; the sketch map used in this study was based on a gross enlargement of a 1:25,000 scale topographic map which was then altered and filled in by the author, based on observations and estimates made by him at the site.

The detailed measurements of the shelters were taken with a ten-meter cloth tape, and were recorded in a field notebook to the nearest centimeter. In quadrilateral rooms, diagonal measurements were taken to check squareness. In nonrectilinear spaces such as the caves, two complete sets of radii were measured from two reference points, and the intersections of these radii were later plotted on paper to establish the key points in the plan. A few vertical measurements and some sketches or photographs usually sufficed for construction of the vertical section drawing.

Two problems arose in the measuring of the various shelters. First, many wall surfaces were sloping, doubly curved, or irregular. In order to simplify the construction of the plan drawings, a convention was followed of taking all measurements at waist level. Second, in the cave monastery at Massafra it was sometimes difficult with the simple equipment at hand to establish the exact spatial relationships among adjacent rooms. Where possible, radii were measured through doorways and a true relationship could be plotted. In some cases, however, educated guesswork had to be employed instead.

The final plans and perspective sections were prepared freehand because it was felt that the freehand line was more descriptive of the true character of the construction than a ruled line. The freehand work was done over accurately constructed pencil layouts. All drawings of shelters were prepared at the metric scale of 1:50, and are reduced in this book to smaller scales. The scheme of plan and perspective section was adopted as being the most descriptive representation which could be reasonably made. Vanishing points for the perspective sections were placed at eye level insofar as possible for greater realism. The orientation of each plan drawing on its page was determined solely by the necessity of preserving an orthographic relationship between it and its most descriptive accompanying section. North directions, except on the maps and town plans, are approximate. In a few buildings very recent structural alterations have been omitted in order to not clutter the drawings. In-town shelters usually have only their interior wall faces represented because it was generally impossible to enter adjacent buildings for the purpose of determining the thicknesses of the party walls, or of the floor and ceiling structures. No attempt has been made to show the internal construction details of walls or vaults, as such details could only have been conjectural. Instead, photographs of various structures in states of partial ruin are furnished to demonstrate typical construction details, and the reader may make his own extrapolations to specific cases.

The photographs were taken by the author except as noted. A 35 mm. Miranda DR was used, with 28 mm., 50 mm., and 135 mm. lenses. Medium yellow and dark red filters were often used for sky or foliage contrast. Kodak Plus-X film was exposed at a rating of A.S.A. 320 and developed in Acufine developer. No artificial lighting was used in any photograph. Although a tripod was used in some cases, the majority of the photographs was taken with the camera hand-held. The ease and rapidity of this technique together with the low cost of the film and the small size of the equipment enabled a spontaneity of picture-taking which could not have occurred with a camera of larger format.

The author was unable to obtain permission from the Italian government to take aerial photographs. A properly licensed aerial photographer wanted eight hundred unavailable dollars for the desired work. The two aerial photographs included in the illustrations were obtained, at outrageous expense and after interminable delays for security clearances, from the Aerofoteca in Rome.

Appendix 2: Notes for the Traveler

The first-time visitor to Italy seldom visits Apulia. The justly famous cities of Venice, Milan, Florence, Pisa, Rome, and Naples are by themselves more than he is able to encompass in one trip. But the seasoned traveler, once he has sampled the delights which present themselves in the span of two hundred miles between Gargano and Santa Maria di Leuca, understands well why the Swabian emperors thought it not ingracious to be known as men of Apulia. And he may begin to suspect that it was more than just the strategic importance of Apulia that caused men of so many nations to risk lives, fortunes, and empires to possess this land, for Apulia is one of those rare corners of the earth which can weave an irresistible and ineradicable spell within a receptive human spirit.

How to get there:

Bari, Brindisi, and the Murgia of the Trulli are all within a comfortable day's drive of Rome. At the time of this writing, the easiest route lies along the Autostrada del Sole from Rome to Caserta Sud, then passes through Benevento, Cerignola, and Canosa, where it enters the autostrada which traverses the olive groves to Bari. New autostrada construction is continually making the journey even easier; the latest maps should always be consulted in order to take advantage of the best possible roads.

An alternative route, somewhat slower, follows the Autostrada del Sole past Naples and the tall cone of Vesuvius, past the beaches of Salerno, now peaceful bathing spots, to Eboli. From Eboli the route leads to Potenza, after which, at Bivio Tricarico, the traveler may decide whether to go to Altamura or to take the southward fork to Matera, a longer but particularly scenic stretch of the Via Appia.

An early start from Rome is advisable, for night driving is extremely hazardous on roads other than the autostrade. Farmers and mulecarts plod slowly and invisibly along the highways after sundown, and large trucks use whatever clear right-of-way is left. Either Benevento or Potenza offers hotels and motels for an overnight stay. Sunday is the best day to make the trip because trucks are not allowed to use the roads, making possible a considerably higher average speed and an infinitely more enjoyable journey.

Apulia is reached by air through the airports at Bari and Brindisi. By sea, coming from Greece, it may be entered at Brindisi or Otranto. Apulia is well served by the Italian national railroads, making it prime territory for holders of Eurailpasses.

Guidebooks:

The Touring Club Italiano picturebook *Attraverso l'Italia: Puglia*, sold at any T.C.I. office (such as the one on Via Sardegna near Via Veneto in Rome), will be useful to even the tourist who does not understand Italian. The T.C.I. guidebook *Guida d'Italia: Puglia*, with its five hundred pages of fine print, is a comprehensive and valuable manual, but only to one with a good reading knowledge of Italian.

Reasonably good English-language tourist guides to Apulia are *Italy No. 9—Apulia, Basilicata, Calabria*, available free of charge from the Ente Nazionale per il Turismo at Via Marghera 6, near Stazione Termini in Rome; and *Puglia*, obtainable without charge from the offices of the Enti Provinciali per il Turismo in Bari, Brindisi, Foggia, Lecce, or Taranto. The office in Bari is at 2 Corso Cavour, and it will mail specific literature on the Bari province. A special E.P.I.T. office next to the city hall in the main square of Alberobello offers special information on the *trulli*, including Mimmo Castellano's delightful book of photographs and essays. When writing or visiting the E.N.I.T. in Rome, incidentally, do not fail to request the introduction to the Italian provincial foods and wines entitled *At Table in Italy*.

The standard English-language tourist guides are of little use in Apulia. The Michelin Green Guide *Italy* carries sketchy descriptions of the major towns, but is neither sufficient nor accurate ("The rooms [of the *trulli*] are roofed with domes of different sizes, each having a central chimney"). The Baedecker is worse yet. Such renowned travelers of Italy as Boswell, Hawthorne, and Berenson have not given us any impressions of Apulia. The Grand Tour almost never went past Naples, unless to Sicily.

Good road maps are available at nominal cost from the Touring Club Italiano. The free maps given at Shell Oil stations in Apulia are equally as good, however, and have information on the various towns printed in four languages on the back, plus map symbols for major scenic routes and tourist attractions.
When to come:
Apulia is hot and dry in the summer, when the *Scirocco* blows steadily from Africa. It can be quite cold and rainy in the winter. May through October are the best months for sightseeing, with the spring and the fall the most delightful because of the moderate temperatures, the abundance of sunlight, and the colors of the countryside.

Except at Brindisi, the gateway to Greece, tourists are scarce in Apulia, helping to make it the best of lands for a vacation. The water of the street fountains, coming cold and clear from the Apennines, is totally fit for consumption by soft-stomached Americans. Hotels and restaurants are not as easy to find as in the heavily traveled North, but are clean, honest, economical, and often of quite good quality. English is seldom spoken, but a genuine desire to communicate on the part of the Apulians often overcomes this barrier, even in restaurants which have no written menu. Waiters will gladly bring samples of the foods of the day to your table to assist you in your choice. Always keep some cash reserve as you travel, for in some untouristed towns even the banks do not recognize travelers' checks. And be prepared to be an object of open curiosity—you may be the first foreigner some unspoiled Apulian has seen.

Sights:
Proceeding clockwise from the north, some of the major points of interest in Apulia are:
Gargano. The famous Padre Pio lived in San Giovanni. At Monte Sant'Angelo is the pilgrimage cave church of the Archangel Michael, dating from the fifth century, filled with beggars but impressive nevertheless. The Foresta Umbra (shady forest) is cherished by tree-poor Italians, but is quite ordinary by American standards. Vieste and Peschici are colorful coastal towns, and the Tremiti Islands are said to be perfect holiday spots, blessed with a picturesque monastery, clear, warm waters for underwater fishing, and extensive sea caves.
Capitanata. A large Swabian castle at Lucera and a Romanesque cathedral at Troia are the major sights. At Canosa, next to the cathedral, is the oddly touching tomb of Boemond, son of Robert Guiscard.
The Adriatic Plain. Some of the finest churches in the world, of Arab-Norman construction, belong to Barletta, Trani, Molfetta (enter through the right-hand transept if the main door is closed), Bitonto, Ruvo, and Bari. These churches are not to be missed! The Trani church is on an unusual and beautiful site, surrounded on three sides by the sea.
    The Dolmen of Bisceglie is just to the east of the autostrada. It can be reached on foot from the eastern (northbound) gasoline station of the autostrada at the Dolmen di Bisceglie oasis, or from Bisceglie by taking the road which appears on the map as the perpendicular bisector of the road between Corato and Ruvo di Puglia, then turning left just before the bridge over the autostrada and following the signs. Other dolmens nearby are virtually impossible for the tourist to find, but the route from Molfetta to the Pulo of Molfetta is well marked. The menhir Monaco di Modugno stands at a crossroads near Modugno—ask a policeman for directions. Throughout this area, along the autostrada and in the endless olive groves, stand thousands of zigguratlike *trullo* shelters. Many stand open and can be easily entered in order to observe the unusual construction and layout.
    Cannae, the site of Hannibal's bloody victory over the Romans, lies between Barletta and Canosa. There is a museum here, and many graves and battlefield sites are marked.
    Bari is a large, cosmopolitan city. Its old town is fascinating to explore and includes a gigantic Swabian castle, a cathedral, and the Church of San Nicola, built to house the saint's remains which were stolen by Barese sailors from Byzantium. Seafood is good here. In the *tavole calde*, a good quick snack is *panzerotto*, a concoction of bread and meat somewhat akin to a folded pizza. At nearby Valenzano is the lovely eleventh-century Chiesa di Ognissanti.
    Going south along the coast from Bari, one encounters scattered *trulli*. A pleasant campground at

San Giorgio Ionico, eleven kilometers from Bari, rents rooms in *trulli* which, though contemporary, are fairly accurate copies of the real thing. Polignano a Mare is a beautiful sea-cliff town, often seen on travel posters as viewed from the highway bridge to the north. It is undercut by extensive sea caves which are open to visitors. At Egnazia are the excavated ruins of a Roman town, clearly visible from the coastal highway. Looking to the southwest one may see the steep flank of the Murgia of the Trulli several miles distant.

Continuing southward along the coast, just past Torre Canne, one passes on the left the campground Pilone, also known as Marina di Ostuni, where a beautiful beach can be used for a very small daily fee. Excellent tennis courts are also available, and luxurious sites for tents and trailers are scattered among the pines.

The Salentine Peninsula. Brindisi still boasts the columns and stair constructed by Trajan in 117 A.D. to mark the end of the Via Appia.

Lecce offers much evidence to support its reputation as the Baroque Florence, as well as a Roman theater in its main square. Many dolmens and menhirs occur in this region, though few are easily found. Dolmen-hunting, both here and in the area north of Bari, is an exciting sport open only to those with much time, patience, and energy, and a fair command of spoken Italian, for it involves frequent stops and expeditions into the fields to ask directions of local farmers.

At Otranto is one of the major marvels of Apulia: a cathedral whose entire floor is a gigantic mosaic tree depicting in its branches the story of the Bible, together with secular and mythological subjects. It dates from 1165.

Along the Salentine coast are found many ruined Saracen watchtowers. At Gallipoli a picturesque island fishing village is connected to the mainland by a long causeway. Curious basket fishtraps are woven here. On the mainland near the end of the causeway is an ancient Greek fountain.

Manduria still retains great megalithic walls along its northern side, remnants of the Messapian defenses. Outside the walls are a moat and thousands of rock-cut Messapian graves. A short distance inside the walls can be found the ancient Fountain of Pliny, a tremendous skylit grotto containing a sacred well.

Taranto is a most exciting town. It is on an island between two large saltwater lagoons, and is a major seaport both for fishing vessels and for the Italian and American navies. Mussels are farmed on the poles seen projecting from the water, and fresh seafood is sold alongside the colorful fishing boats on the inland side of the island. Sea urchins can be eaten raw on the spot, seasoned with lemon juice. Across the street from the docks are many good restaurants; their *zuppa di pesce* is one of the most delightful and surprising dishes of Italy. The Museo Nazionale of Taranto houses thousands of vases, pieces of jewelry, household articles, and sculptures from Magna Graecia, and many excellent finds from the pre-Greek eras. To the west, at Metaponto, are located the ruins of a Greek temple and a free museum containing relics and information pertaining to the important Greek colony on that site.

The Murgia of the Trulli. Alberobello is the center of the region of the *trulli*, and has a relatively heavy tourist traffic. Two quarters of the town are preserved in their original state. Small children will ask persistently if you want to see a *trullo*. Go with them and tour their family home, then pay them 50 to 100 *lire* for the tour. Some gift shops are housed in *trulli* and can be viewed at no cost. The wool bedspreads on sale in the lower *piazza* are a good buy, but haggle awhile, then start to walk away if the price does not suit you. The Hotel dei Trulli and the Tourist Village at the top of the Rione Monti are both first class, expensive, and phoney. The Cucina dei Trulli, in Piazza Ferdinando IV, just off Piazza del Popolo, the main square of the new town, has clean, sunny double rooms with toilets at very reasonable prices. Its dining room, which has no printed menu, serves the local wines and special dishes without pretense. Chilled *vino rosato* is especially good to drink. *Purea di fave con verdura* is served as a first course every Friday noon, and is worth building your travel schedule around. If you are within fifty miles of Alberobello on a Friday, drive in to taste this peasant dish. Other good first courses are *orecchiette* and the thickest *minestrone* you will ever eat. *Pasta piselli*, pasta with peas, is available in season. Good second courses include *involtini al sugo* (veal rolls in sauce), *fegato* (tender beef liver), and *vitello arrosto* (roast veal with oil and herbs).

Cisternino is almost entirely untouristed, except by Italians from surrounding communities who enjoy the cool breeziness of its lofty location during the heat of the summer. The old town is fascinating with its outdoor staircases, vaulted underpasses, and serpentine streets too narrow for cars. At the western edge of town one may relax under pines or palms and view the fabulous Valley of Itria, a hundred square miles of vineyards sprinkled with *trulli*. In the first block of Via Regina Margherita as it drops away from the old town toward the southeast is found the Ristorante Da Bina. Here one can sample Bina's home cooking, sometimes *purea di fave*, but more often succulent, meat-filled *pasta al forno*, rich *minestrone*, *orecchiette*, *polpettoni* (large meatballs), and *gnumaredd*—tiny, tasty rolls of lamb entrails. Wines of the Valley of Itria are served. Son Niccolo speaks English. Uphill and just around the corner to the left is a basement bar where cones of delicious homemade ice cream are available for pennies. Unfortunately there is no hotel or *pensione* in Cisternino, although Bina's family may start one soon.

Fourteen kilometers from Cisternino is Ostuni, a town most notable for its dazzling external appearance, best seen from the road which winds down the flank of the Murgia to the north of town. Almost totally whitewashed and with much of its medieval wall intact, it is known as the White Queen of the Olives.

Martina Franca has a palace by Bernini, and its wall-encircled old town contains many interesting streets and baroque-detailed houses. From its municipal garden another fine view of the Valley of Itria can be enjoyed. Several hotels and restaurants are available. The roads radiating from Martina to Cisternino, Ceglie Messapico, Villa Castelli, Taranto, Massafra, Alberobello, and Locorotondo traverse some of the most photogenic *trullo* areas of the Murgia.

At the southern edge of the Murgia, Grottaglie is a famous center for the making of pottery. Yellow signs lead to the ceramicists' quarter where thousands of finished pots are piled high on rooftops. Utilitarian pots in brown and cream glazes are extremely cheap at any of the shops. At the Ceramica Fasano, one can see pots being thrown by hand, then fired in an immense furnace stoked with olive branches and ground olive pits.

At Massafra are many frescoed Byzantine cave chapels which may be toured in the company of a guide obtained from the city hall. Going straight north from the old town and bearing left at the fork with the roadside shrine, park the car, descend the steps by the church of the Madonna della Scala, and walk up the ravine to explore the deserted cave community described in Chapter 3. Hiking clothes are recommended. You are on your own here—no guides, no admission charge, no explanatory signs.

Matera is a partially occupied cave town, much larger and more impressive than Massafra. The Strada dei Sassi may be followed by car or on foot for spectacular views of the town and the ravine. On the other side of the ravine are many isolated caves, some of which date from the Stone Age.

Noci, Locorotondo, and Putignano are still in the heart of the region of the *trulli*. At Castellana Grotte and Putignano are great limestone caverns which have been developed for tourism. These are typical of the labyrinth of underground passages which drain the Murgia.

The new tourist road from Castellana Grotte to Selva di Fasano skirts the very edge of the Murgia, offering spectacular views toward the sea while passing by some of the finest *trulli* in the region. Selva di Fasano, once one of the most fascinating areas of the Murgia, is now becoming a fairly flossy vacation community. On the back roads in a triangle bounded by Selva di Fasano, Locorotondo, and Cisternino, numerous tiny *trullo* towns are found, some more or less intact and others spoiled by new construction. If one stays on the main gravel roads, there is small danger in spending a leisurely hour or two exploring this little known area. Beware of any road which shows no tire tracks, however, unless you are driving an underfed Land Rover.

Trulli are for sale all over the Murgia, often for a few hundred dollars. Should you come to feel that you cannot do without one of your own, it is advisable to have an Italian bargain for its acquisition, without your name or nationality being made known to the seller.

The Northern Murgia. The only important tourist sight is the jewel-like octagonal Castel del Monte which was the hunting lodge of Frederick II. It crowns a hill above a plain dotted with *trullo* shelters, now abandoned, and is one of the most striking architectural monuments in Italy.

Epilogue:

These notes are a bare listing of a few things discovered during the course of the studies on which this book is based. They cannot be complete, for Apulia is one of the best endowed and least known vacation areas of Europe. The traveler is encouraged to obtain all available literature in the provincial capitals, and to make up his own itinerary. Better still, he should simply explore, take the roads which look most interesting, and enjoy the thrill of discovery which is still possible in this unspoiled land.

Notes

I

1. Berkeley's favorite among the Apulian cities was Lecce. See Alice Brayton, *George Berkeley in Apulia* (Boston: Merrymount Press, 1946).

2. "Carsici, fenomeni," *Enciclopedia Italiana*, IX, 173.

3. On Grotto Romanelli: Ernst Pulgram, *The Tongues of Italy* (Cambridge, Mass.: Harvard University Press, 1958), p. 98; Torre Testa: Quirico Punzi, "Torre Testa, stazione preistorica costiera del Brindisino," estratto da *Ricerche e Studi*, Quaderno n. 3, Anno 1967, Museo F. Ribezzo, Brindisi; trade between Apulia and the countries of the Aegean: Touring Club Italiano, *Guida d'Italia: Puglia* (Milano: 1962), p. 27; population of the Murgia and first colonization: for this information the author is indebted to Dott. Quirico Punzi of Cisternino.

4. Earliest tribes: Osvaldo Baldacci, *Puglia* (Torino: Editrice Torinese, 1962), pp. 22, 23; descent of Messapians from the Illyrians: E. T. Salmon, *Samnium and the Samnites* (Cambridge: At the University Press, 1967), p. 58; Salentine Peninsula and Calabria: Touring Club Italiano, *Puglia*, p. 27.

5. Mycenaeans: A. G. Woodhead, *The Greeks in the West* (New York: Frederick A. Praeger, 1962), p. 21. Dott. Quirico Punzi has confirmed the existence of Mycenaean colonies on the Adriatic shore; Taranto: Woodhead, *Greeks*, pp. 64, 65; Greek control: Touring Club Italiano, *Puglia*, p. 28.

6. Woodhead, *Greeks*, p. 100.

7. Campaigns of 307-302 B.C. and 296 B.C.: Salmon, *Samnium*, pp. 246-248, 257, 263; campaigns of 326 and 299 B.C.: Touring Club Italiano, *Puglia*, p. 28.

8. Woodhead, *Greeks*, p. 105.

9. Via Appia: R. J. Forbes, *Ancient Roads* (Amsterdam: Adolph M. Hakkert, 1964), p. 123; trade from ports: Touring Club Italiano, *Puglia*, pp. 28, 29.

10. For the history of Apulia from 218 B.C. through the ninth century A.D., the author is indebted to the Touring Club Italiano's *Puglia*, pp. 29, 30, 152.

11. For the Norman history of Apulia, the author is indebted to C. A. Willemsen and D. Odenthal's *Apulia, Imperial Splendor in Southern Italy*, translated from the German by Daphne Woodward (New York: Frederick A. Praeger, 1959), pp. 11-18.

12. From the Hohenstaufen rule to the 1860 vote for unification, see Touring Club Italiano, *Puglia*, pp. 31-33.

13. Pulgram, *Tongues of Italy*, p. 50.

II

1. Michele Gervasio, *I dolmen e la civiltà del bronzo nelle Puglie* (Bari: Commissione Provinciale di Archeologia e Storia Patria, 1913), pp. 311 ff.

2. For this information the author is indebted to Dott. Quirico Punzi of Cisternino.

3. *Ibid.*

4. Matera: T. Eric Peet, *The Stone and Bronze Ages in Italy and Sicily* (Oxford: Clarendon Press, 1909), p. 108; Molfetta: Maximilian Mayer, *Molfetta und Matera* (Leipzig: Verlag Karl W. Hiersemann, 1924); road at Molfetta: Forbes, *Ancient Roads*, p. 34.

5. Gervasio, *I dolmen*, p. 47.

6. The Dolmen of Bisceglie and the Dolmen of Albarosa: David Trump, *Central and Southern Italy Before Rome* (London: Thames and Hudson, 1966), pp. 226 and 145; the Tavola dei Paladini and Cisternino dolmen: Antonio Jatta, *La Puglia preistorica* (Bari: Commissione Provinciale di Archeologia e Storia Patria, 1914), pp. 151 and 68.

7. Dolmens of the Salentine peninsula: Trump, *Italy Before Rome*, pp. 87, 88, and 226.

8. Jatta, *La Puglia preistorica*, pp. 144-147.

9. Number of menhirs still existing: Giuseppe Notarnicola, *I trulli di Alberobello* (Roma: Unione Editoriale d'Italia, 1940), p. 5; function of menhirs and attitude of Christian church: Gervasio, *I dolmen*, pp. 346, 347; Corsican menhirs: "Stone Men of Corsica," *Time*, July 12, 1968, p. 70.

10. Date of burial *specchie*: David Randall-MacIver, *The Iron Age in Italy* (Oxford: Clarendon Press, 1927), pp. 241, 242; contents of: Trump, *Italy Before Rome*, pp. 152, 153.

11. Lack of contents of defense *specchie*: Trump, *Italy Before Rome*, pp. 152, 153; underlying structure of: *Studi Salentini*, December 1956, pp. 74-84; Il Paretone: Dott. Quirico Punzi.

12. Trump, *Italy Before Rome*, p. 226.

13. Jatta, *La Puglia preistorica*, pp. 222, 223.

14. Egyptian and Mesopotamian vaulting: Giorgio Simoncini, *Architettura contadina di Puglia* (Genova: Vitale e Ghianda, 1960), p. 17; Greek tholos form: Enzo Minchilli, "I trulli di Puglia," in *La valle dei Trulli*, Mimmo Castellano, ed. (Bari: Ente Provinciale per il Turismo, 1959), p. 109; Sardinian *nuraghi*: Peet, *Stone and Bronze Ages*, pp. 225-231.

15. Pasquale Maggiulli, *Specchie e trulli in Terra d'Otranto* (Lecce: Tipografia Editrice Leccese E. Bortone e Comp., 1909).

16. Pietro Lippolis, *Alberobello* (Roma: Istituto Grafico Tiberino, 1961), pp. 32, 33.

17. Gino Chierici, "Il trullo," *Atti del IX Congresso Nazionale di Storia dell'Architettura*, Bari 1955, p. 207.

18. Simoncini, *Architettura contadina di Puglia*, p. 12.

III

1. Hundreds of abandoned *vicinanze* still exist in the older portions of Massafra. The typical form consists of a rectangular central courtyard sunk a level below the surrounding terrain, with three to nine houses excavated around and opening onto the courtyard. Unfortunately the existence of these dwelling clusters did not come to the author's attention until after the field work for this project had been completed, so drawings and photographs of them could not be included in this volume. See Espedito Jacovelli, *S. Maria della Scala di Massafra* (Massafra: Tipografia Fratelli di Lorenzo, 1963), p. 15. For repopulation of Messapha: Jacovelli, *S. Maria*, p. 9.

2. Espedito Jacovelli, *Gli affreschi bizantini di Massafra* (Massafra: Pro Loco di Massafra, 1960), p. 7.

3. Bertha Diener, *Imperial Byzantium* (Boston: Little, Brown and Co., 1938), p. 134.

4. Population of the Madonna della Scala: Jacovelli, *Gli affreschi bizantini*, p. 8; function of monastery: Jacovelli, *S. Maria*, p. 58; language and religion: Charles Diehl, *Byzantium: Greatness and Decline* (New Brunswick, N.J.: Rutgers University Press, 1957), p. 78.

5. Jacovelli, *S. Maria*, p. 58, and *Gli affreschi bizantini*, p. 8.

6. Function of Grotto of Cyclops: Jacovelli, *S. Maria*, p. 51; function of paths: *Ibid.*, p. 52; crypt churches: Touring Club Italiano, *Puglia*, pp. 285, 286.

7. Jacovelli, *Gli affreschi bizantini*, p. 17.

8. Henry David Thoreau, *Walden*, in *Walden and Other Writings of Henry David Thoreau* (New York: The Modern Library, 1950), pp. 34, 35.

IV

1. Mariano Marraffa, *I trulli di Alberobello* (Roma: Editrice Adriana, 1960), pp. 13-18. This Selva has no connection with the present-day town of Selva di Fasano.

2. Inducements to immigrants and increase in population: Notarnicola, *I trulli*, pp. 155 and 249; settlers from across Adriatic: V. Ricchioni, "Aspetti della trasformazione fondiaria nella Murgia dei Trulli," *Atti del XVII Congresso Geografico Italiano* (Bari: Editore Cressati, 1957), II, 333.

3. Simoncini, *Architettura contadina di Puglia*, p. 37.

4. Oronzo Sisto and Gino Angiulli, *Alberobello, la città dei trulli* (Putignano: De Robertis, 1961), p. 10.

5. *Ibid.*, p. 7.

6. Notarnicola, *I trulli*, p. 43. Another story would have it that the Count wanted to be able to demolish any house as punishment to its owner; see Sisto and Angiulli, *Alberobello*, p. 7.

7. Notarnicola, *I trulli*, pp. 228, 229.

8. Marraffa, *I trulli*, pp. 42-44.

9. Eighteenth-century development of Selva: Notarnicola, *I trulli*, p. 248; population estimate: there is some doubt about the accuracy of this figure, which is given by Sisto and Angiulli, *Alberobello*, p. 12. Notarnicola on p. 265 lists a population of 3,200 for the same year. On pp. 23 and 24 of Sisto and Angiulli the present population of the two remaining *trullo* quarters of Alberobello is given as 4,500, which would imply that considerable growth took place after 1797; clandestine meeting: Marraffa, *I trulli*, p. 57.

10. Sisto and Angiulli, *Alberobello*, pp. 12, 13, and Marraffa, *I trulli*, p. 57.

11. Sisto and Angiulli, *Alberobello*, p. 14.

12. Notarnicola, *I trulli*, p. 61.

13. For this information the author is indebted to Geometro Vincenzo Punzi and Mr. Vincent Scarafile of Cisternino.

14. Land preparation: Ricchioni, "Aspetti della trasformazione," pp. 338-340. See also Lippolis,

Alberobello, pp. 135, 136, and Michele Palmieri, *Bari e la Puglia* (Bari: Editoriale Adda, 1964), p. 183; fertilization: Paul Wilstach, "The Stone Beehive Homes of the Italian Heel," *National Geographic Magazine*, Feb. 1930, p. 259.

15. For this information the author is indebted to Ingegner Giovanni Sabatino of Cisternino.

16. Notarnicola, *I trulli*, p. 117.

17. Marraffa, *I trulli*, pp. 92 and 96.

18. Saverino La Sorsa, "Significato simbolico dei trulli," *Atti del Congresso di Studi Etnografici Italiani* (Napoli: R. Pironti e Figli, 1952), pp. 180-185.

19. Sun symbols: Simoncini, *Architettura contadina di Puglia*, p. 35; ciphers of Christ and Mary: Giuseppe Cocchiara, "Il trullo, tra magia e religione," in *La valle dei trulli*, pp. 91-103; swastika: La Sorsa, "Significato simbolico dei Trulli," pp. 180-185.

V

1. Cisternino, unlike Massafra and Alberobello, has never had its history recorded in print. This is not because of a lack of local interest. Both Dott. Quirico Punzi and the priest Saverio Ostuni have written valuable historical monographs about Cisternino, but neither has been successful in finding a publisher. Virtually all the historical information in this chapter was related to the author by these two scholars. Occasionally their separate accounts do not agree precisely. In this instance, Dott. Punzi gives the name of the original monastery as San Nicolo di Patara, whereas Sac. Ostuni records it as San Nicola di Mira.

2. Geometro Vincenzo Punzi states that the vaulting of Cisternino was generally erected with wooden centering, and his statement is borne out by the author's observations. In other parts of Apulia there is a tradition of building uncentered vaults; see Saul Greco, *Muri, volte, e case di Puglia* (Milano: Istituto Propaganda Internazionale, 1954).

3. This information also comes from Geom. Punzi.

VI

1. In Alberobello alone one-third of the population were issued visas to emigrate between 1900 and 1910. See Lippolis, *Alberobello*, p. 84. Probably the most famous emigrant from the Murgia of the Trulli was a young man of Castellaneta who went to Hollywood to seek his fortune. His name was Rodolfo Valentino.

Glossary

Acquedotto Pugliese. The modern acqueduct which supplies Apulia with water from the Apennine Mountains.

Apuli. The Latin name for the Iapygians.

Bolo. A red soil rich in hydroxides of iron and calcium which is found in depressions in the limestone surface of a *murgia.*

Capanna. A primitive shelter with a wooden roof structure. Plural *capanne.*

Casedda, casella. A type of *trullo* shelter built along the Adriatic coast of Apulia. Sometimes applied to other types of stone farmhouses as well. Plurals *casedde, caselle.*

Chiancarelle, chianche, chiancole. The flat limestone pieces used in many types of Apulian shelters for roofing or paving.

Chipuro, chipuru. A type of *trullo* shelter built in the Salentine Peninsula. Plural *chipuri.*

Cucina a terra. An open fireplace used for cooking.

Cucurneo. The decorative finial of a *trullo.*

Daunia. The ancient land which occupied the northern part of Apulia.

Gargano Massif. The spur of Italy, a mountainous peninsula which projects into the Adriatic Sea from northern Apulia.

Gravina. A dry ravine in the *tufo* area of the southern Murgia of the Trulli. When capitalized in this text, refers to the Gravina of the Madonna della Scala of Massafra. Plural *gravine.*

Iapygia. Daunia and Peucetia.

Imbianchino. One who whitewashes buildings.

Murgia. A limestone plateau with subterranean drainage, without rivers, streams, ponds, or lakes. When capitalized in this text, refers to the Murgia of the Trulli. Pronounced MOOR-jah. Plural *murge.*

Messapia. The ancient land of the Messapians (*Messapi* in Italian), which consisted mainly of the Salentine Peninsula.

Nuraghe. A type of *trullo* structure, thought to have been defensive in purpose, found in large numbers on the island of Sardinia. Plural *nuraghi.*

Pagghiaro, pagghiaru. A type of stone-walled shelter with a roof of wood and straw which is found on the northern edge of the Murgia of the Trulli. Plural *pagghiari.*

Paretone. The stone wall which once divided Messapia from Peucetia.

Peucetia. The ancient land of the Peucetians (*Peucezi* in Italian), which occupied the central portion of Apulia.

Puglia. The Italian name for Apulia, pronounced POOL-yah. *Fortunata terra di Puglia,* fortunate land of Apulia.

Rione Aia Piccola, Rione Monti. The two quarters of Alberobello which are preserved as national monuments.

Salentine Peninsula. The heel of Italy, called *Peninsola Salentina* or *Salento* in Italian.

Selva. Literally, a forest. The name of the original settlement on the site now occupied by Alberobello.

Selvese. An inhabitant of the Selva. Plural *selvesi.*

Solaio. The attic platform in a *trullo* dome.

Specchia. A rock cairn, for either defensive or funerary purposes. Plural *specchie.*

Suma. A measure of wine. One *suma* consists of twelve *mezzi* of eleven liters each.

Tavolato. A *solaio.*

Tintinule. A dialect term for the decorative pinnacle of a *trullo.*

Trudd, truddo, truddu. Dialect forms of *trullo.*

Trullo. A type of structure having a conical vault of unmortared, corbelled stone, of the refined type of construction that is found in the vicinity of Alberobello. Pronounced TROOL-low with an Italian *R.* Plural *trulli,* pronounced TROOL-lee.

Trullo shelter. A term used in this book to denote a structure with a conical vault of unmortared stone which does not possess all the refinements of a *trullo.*

Tufo. A soft, homogeneous sedimentary rock composed mainly of volcanic detritus.

Vicinanza. Literally, *neighborhood.* A cluster of manmade cave houses opening to a sunken communal courtyard which is excavated from a horizontal surface of *tufo.*

Selected References

Allen, Edward. "Cisternino in Puglia," *L'architettura, cronache e storia*, December 1967, pp. 544-549.

Baldacci, Osvaldo. *Puglia*. Torino: Editrice Torinese, 1962.

Battaglia, Raffaello. "Osservazioni sulla distribuzione e sulla forma dei trulli Pugliesi," *Archivio Storico Pugliese*, December 1952, pp. 34-44.

Benincasa, Eglo. "L'arte di abitare nel mezzogiorno," *L'architettura, cronache e storia*: "Il colore," May-June 1955, pp. 58-65; "Vita all'aperto," July-August 1955, pp. 240-245; "Inno al rustico," September-October 1955, pp. 392-397; "La deformazione," November-December 1955, pp. 564-567; "Barocco minore," January-February 1956, pp. 716-720; "Gli ambienti," March-April 1956, pp. 874-878.

Bertacchi, C. "Nella Puglia Pietrosa," *Iapigia*, Vol. XI, Nos. 1-2, pp. 5-26.

Berucci, Mario. "Considerazioni sulle pseudo-volte," *Atti del IX Congresso Nazionale di Storia dell'-Architettura*. Bari: 1955, pp. 209-214.

Brandi, Cesare. *Pellegrino di Puglia*. Bari: Editori Laterza, 1960.

Castellano, Mimmo. *La valle dei trulli*. Bari: Ente Provinciale per il Turismo, 1959.

Charney, Melvin. "The Trulli of Southern Italy," *Landscape*, Autumn 1965, p. 32.

Chierici, Gino, "Il trullo," *Atti del IX Congresso Nazionale di Storia dell'Architettura*. Bari: 1955, pp. 203-207.

Circolo La Scaletta. *Le chiese rupestri di Matera*. Roma: De Luca Editore, 1966.

Gallo, Vincenzo. *Origine e vicende della città di Massafra*. Napoli: Officina Cromotipografica Aldina, 1916.

Gervasio, Michele. *I dolmen e la civiltà del bronzo*. Bari: Commissione Provinciale di Archeologia e Storia Patria, 1913.

Greco, Saul. *Muri, volte, e case di Puglia*. Milano: Istituto Propaganda Internazionale, 1954.

Jacovelli, Espedito. *Gli affreschi bizantini di Massafra*. Massafra: Tipografia Fratelli di Lorenzo, 1960.
————. *S. Maria della Scala di Massafra*. Massafra: Tipografia Fratelli di Lorenzo, 1963.

Jatta, Antonio. *La Puglia preistorica*. Bari: Commissione Provinciale di Archeologia e Storia Patria, 1914.

La Sorsa, Saverino. *Storia di Puglia*. 6 vols. Bari: Tipografia Levante, 1953–1962.

"La valle dei trulli," *Architectural Review*, December 1960, pp. 420 ff.

Lilliu, Giovanni. *I Nuraghi—Torri preistoriche di Sardegna*. Cagliari: Edizioni La Zattera, 1962.

Lippolis, Pietro. *Alberobello*. Roma: Istituto Grafico Tiberino, 1961.

Marraffa, Mariano. *I trulli di Alberobello*. Roma: Editrice Tipografica Adriana, 1960.

Mayer, Maximilian. *Molfetta und Matera*. Leipzig: Verlag Karl W. Hiersemann, 1924.

Minchilli, Enzo. "Martina Franca," *Casabella 209*, January-February 1956, pp. 47-49.

Notarnicola, Giuseppe. *I trulli di Alberobello*. Roma: Unione Editoriale d'Italia, 1940.

Palmieri, Michele. *Bari e la Puglia*. Bari: Editoriale Adda, 1964.

Palumbo, Giuseppe. "Salento megalitico," *Studi Salentini*. June 1956, pp. 58-73.

Peet, T. Eric. *The Stone and Bronze Ages in Italy and Sicily*. Oxford: Clarendon Press, 1909.

Rudofsky, Bernardo. "Architettura senza architetto: In Puglia," *Domus*, No. 431 (1965), pp. 52-54.

Simoncini, Giorgio. *Architettura contadina di Puglia*. Genova: Vitali e Ghianda, 1960.

————. "Edilizia rustica di Puglia," *Quaderni dell'Istituto di Storia dell'Architettura*, Serie VI, VII, VIII, Fascicoli da 31 a 48 (1961), pp. 347-352.

Sisto, Oronzo, and Gino Angiulli. *Alberobello, la città dei trulli*. Putignano: De Robertis, 1961.

Touring Club Italiano. *Attraverso l'Italia: Puglia*. Milano: 1967.

————. *Guida d'Italia: Puglia*. Milano: 1962.

Trump, David. *Central and Southern Italy Before Rome*. London: Thames and Hudson, 1966.

Willemsen, C. A., and D. Odenthal. *Apulia, Imperial Splendor in Southern Italy*. Translated by Daphne Woodward. New York: Frederick A. Praeger, 1959.

Index